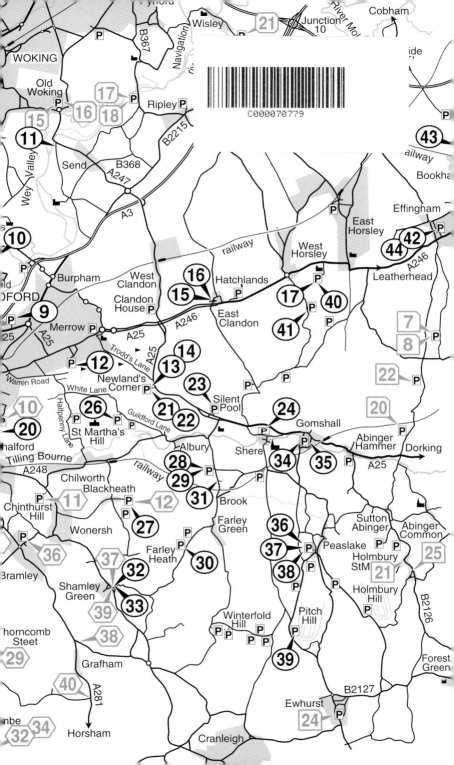

1 Pirbright and Fox Corner

10.2 km/6¼ miles, divisible into walks of 6.9 km/4¼ miles & 6.0 km/3¾ miles
mostly level, woods and fields on the Bagshot Sands; fairly shady, boggy part
in wet seasons. OS maps 1:25000 145 Guildford, 1:50000 186 Aldershot.

Start from Pirbright car park on the village green, SU 946 561, or from Fox
Corner, SU 963 548, where the cul-de-sac, Berry Lane, has kerbside parking.
Useful for the short walks is parking in Bullswater Common Road, SU 953 54

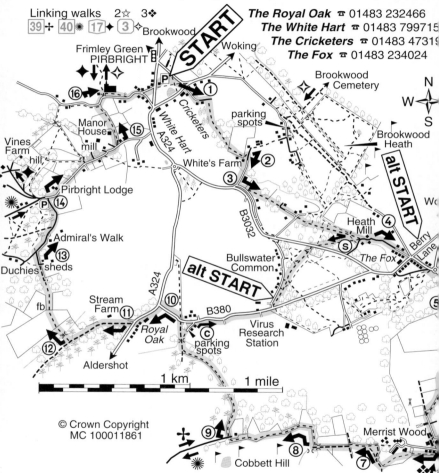

Linking walks   2☆ 3❖
39✚ 40✳ 17◆ 3◇ Brookwood

The Royal Oak ☎ 01483 232466
The White Hart ☎ 01483 799715
The Cricketers ☎ 01483 47319
The Fox ☎ 01483 234024

① Cross Pirbright village green
towards the *Cricketers* (200m).
and follow the drive L of it through
the nursery, round L to a footpath
R (200m). Take the path through
the trees (300m) and over the field
to the far R corner (200m).

② On the lane turn R past
White's Farm to the road (250m).
③ Turn L on the side road (100m)
then diverge L on the path behind
gardens (250m). Stay ahead on th
drive, over a lane and through tree
to the track with houses (550m).

2

Shorter walk: 6.9 km/4¾ miles:
ırn back R on the diverging path
the road (300m). Slightly R cross
to Bullswater Common and stay
ıead on the main path to the next
ad (500m). Cross out of the side
ad to the pavement and turn R
ıst the Virus Research Institute.
eep on to the cross path after the
ext cluster of houses (600m). ➔⑩

) Go L, over the brook at Heath
ill, and ahead to the road at Fox
orner (400m). Cross and follow
e R pavement ahead (200m),
ıst the roundabout and over the
ook to the first field R (300m). ☆

) Cross the field obliquely L up
wards the top corner (150m). Go
ı between fields to Merrist Wood
ollege (600m), along the drive
50m) and R&L between buildings
the main drive (100m). ❖✢

) Cross to the field fence and turn
along it. Keep on past the corner
Merrist Wood house down to the
ottom corner of the garden (350m).

) Outside the garden turn R to
e wood (150m) and go L down
e path beside it (150m). Carry on
head at the farm track (250m).

) After the bridge turn R along the
ath near the brook (150m) then L
long the golf course fence through
ıe fields until past the house R
ehind garden hedge) (400m). ✷

) Turn R across the drive. Stay
head, beside the garden, and join
ıe path from L (750m). Bear R
nd cross the stream (80m).

) *Shorter walk: 6 km/3¾ miles:*
Bear R past the houses to the road
150m). Follow the pavement R
500m). After the Virus Research
ıstitute turn L on the side road
20m) and R into Bullswater
Common. Follow the path ahead to the B3032 (500m). Cross (20m R) and take the diverging path through the trees to the houses (300m). ➔④

⑩ Join the road ahead (120m) and follow the pavement L to the A324. (200m). Turn L (150m). After the ***Royal Oak*** (50m), cross the road to the forest track L of the farm drive.

⑪ Follow the track at the edge of the wood L past the farm R (150m) and the next field (200m). After it (100m) watch for the side path R.

⑫ Follow the side path under trees and between fields (500m) then the cart track ahead up past sheds R to a major vehicle track (200m).

⑬ Turn R up the track round the end of the hill to the road or zigzag over the hill on footpaths trending in the same direction (400m). ✦

⑭ Walk along the road R, past Pirbright Lodge L, to the ponds at Manor Farm L (400m) and over the mill tail bridge (200m).

⑮ Turn L on the drive next to the drive of Pirbright Manor (30m) and continue across the fields at the R edge (300m). Join the lane to Pirbright Church R (100m). ✧

⑯ Turn L over the footbridge (30m) and R though the churchyard past the galetted heathstone tower to Stanley's grave (a tall granite lump) near the far end (200m). Continue on the lane to the village green (400m). Cross via the village (Lord Pirbright's) hall to the public car park behind it (200m).

The **Virus Research Institute** was founded in 1914 for cow tuberculosis and is now known for Foot & Mouth. It is the national laboratory for viruses of farm animals. Strains are identified and spread investigated. Strategies for control are developed and tested.

2 Whitmoor Common and Worplesdon

About 7.3 km/4½ miles with an extension of 1 km/²/₃ mile; heath and fields; one gentle hill; half shady; a welly walk in wet winters. The paths on the commons are confusing. OS maps 1:25000 145 Guildford, 1:50000 186 Aldershot.

Start from Whitmoor Common car park, SU 981 529, or from the cul de sac next to the White Lyon, SU 970 534, or, on the extension, from the public car park on Burdenshott Road, next to the *Jolly Farmer*, SU 987 542.

Linking walks   1☆ 3✿ 39❂

White Lyon & Dragon ☎ 01483 698440
The Jolly Farmer ☎ 01483 235897
Worplesdon Place ☎ 01483 232407

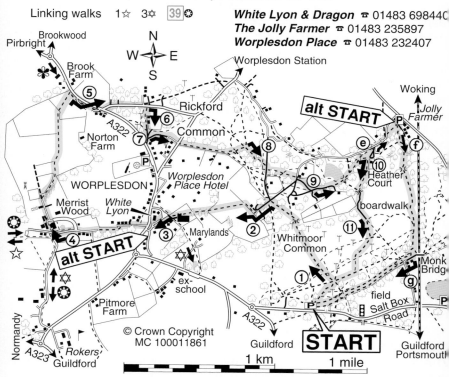

© Crown Copyright MC 100011861

At Whitmoor Common car park take the path away from the road at the R corner to the 6-way junction (200m). Turn on the 2nd L. ① Follow the path through open heath to the stream (500m). Soon after the footbridge, fork L to the vehicle cross track (200m). ② Go L to the house (100m). At the bend take the path ahead, L of the drive. Turn R along the hedge behind the garden (80m) then cross the field L to the top corner (250m).

Keep on up through the trees into Worplesdon churchyard. ✿ Find the semaphore stone on the side path opposite the east end of the church then go on to the lych gate (200m). ③ Outside, turn L beside the hedge and keep on down the narrow drive (100m). Cross the A322, L of the **White Lyon**, and go down the drive opposite, L of the green. Continue through the grounds of Merrist Wood College as far as the main drive which descends L (650m).✿❂

4

From the junction, take the path between the buildings (80m). ⟩rn R (20m) then L along the farm ⟩ve (150m). Bear R on the path at ⟩ fields. Carry on between fields ⟩0m), into a field and across to ⟩ A322 at the far L corner (150m).

⟩ Turn R on the pavement (200m) ⟩d L up Goose Rye Road (300m).

⟩ Just after to the shared tarmac ⟩ve L (20m), take the path R up ⟩o the trees and past a garden ⟩ll (200m). Continue on the drive ⟩m the house (100m).

⟩ Turn L round the houses on the ⟩st track before the road. At the ⟩rmac drive, descend to the road ⟩200m). Cross and go straight up ⟩ the path under the trees (300m).

⟩On top, fork L on the path round the brow of Jordan Hill, past one ⟩ross path (50m) to the 2nd (70m).

⑧ Turn R down the hillside to the ⟩major track (200m). Make for the ⟩ house ahead, ie R then first L ⟩ (250m). Take the track R of the ⟩house to the cross track (100m).

⟩ Turn L (150m). At the R bend ⟩efore the house bear L on the ⟩th to Brook Pond (80m). After the ⟩idge (50m) ignore a ½L path and ⟩in the path converging L (100m). ⟩oon after that (20m), fork R to ⟩e corner of Heather Court (40m).

ⓔ *Extension of 1 km/²/₃ mile: Turn L to the road (100m) and follow it R (120m). Just round the L bend take the path R over the grass towards the public car park next to the **Jolly Farmer** (100m).*

ⓕ *Outside the car park is a vehicle track and next to that a path. Turn S on the path into the trees (100m) and fork L to the stream (200m). Carry on near the railway (Woking - Guildford line) (400m), to the track from Monkey Bridge crossing the railway (200m).*

ⓖ *Turn R past the houses (100m). At the bend in the lane stay ahead on one of the paths outside the field L (450m). After the field continue ahead to the car park (200m).*

⑩ Turn R on the path beside the garden and carry on to the path junction near the stream (200m). Turn L over the footbridge and follow the long boardwalk over a boggy part of the heath (200m).

⑪ At the end of the boardwalk bear R on the main path to the junction (100m). Carry on, under small power lines (50m), to the next cross path (120m). Stay ahead to the next cross path (70m) and turn R to the 6-way junction (150m). Take the 2nd L for the car park (200m) or the 2nd R to carry on. ➜①

⟩he **Admiralty Semaphore Tower** at ⟩Vorplesdon was the tallest station and ⟩nuch taller than the church. It was built ⟩ 1825 as the first in the Plymouth ⟩ranch line from Chatley Heath tower ⟩vhich already served Portsmouth and ⟩vhich still stands overlooking the M25. ⟩he line closed down in 1831 before ⟩completion which would explain the ⟩ibsence of a signal mast. The tower ⟩vas pulled down in 1859 and its site ⟩idded to the churchyard. The picture ⟩s reproduced from a woodcut of 1845.

3 Worplesdon, Littlefield Manor & Merrist Wood

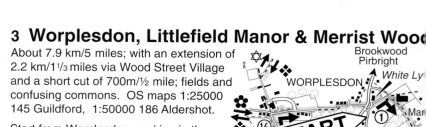

About 7.9 km/5 miles; with an extension of 2.2 km/1⅓ miles via Wood Street Village and a short cut of 700m/½ mile; fields and confusing commons. OS maps 1:25000 145 Guildford, 1:50000 186 Aldershot.

Start from Worplesdon, parking in the cul-de-sac near the *White Lyon*, SU 970 534, or, on the extension, from Wood Street Village behind the green, SU 953 509.

Linking 1❖ 2✿ 4❀ 5★ 6♣ 7♣ 39 ❖

White Lyon & Dragon 01483 698440
Rokers Restaurant 01483 330057

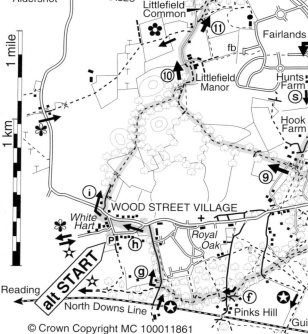

① Walk up the drive R of the ***White Lyon*** to <u>Worplesdon</u> church (150m). Cross the churchyard ahead from the lychgate to the field (150m). Go down the R edge, over the drive (not a RoW), L of the pond and across the A322 (350m).
② Go R on the pavement (200m). After the former school turn L up

the tarmac drive (200m). Enter the field at the end and follow the hedge R to the road (250m).

③ Walk down the road L (350m).
④ After the footpath R and the next houses, turn down the footpath L (350m). Just before the pond strike out R across the grass to the A323 (300m) and go L on the pavement (200m).
⑤ After the house L, cross into the drive of the next house and skirt th

6

rden to the next road (100m).
rn L to the roundabout (20m), L
o Broadstreet Common and R
ong the edge, past the road
nd, to Hunts Farm drive (150m).

Short cut of 700m/½ mile:
oss the drive and follow the
undary path, outside the field, to
ok Farm (400m). Stay ahead on
e vehicle track to the R bend
00m) then on the footpath forking
(100m). Bear R on the side path
the fence corner (30m). →⑨

Turn L on the drive and watch
t for the path R in the trees
20m). Follow the path to open
assland (100m) and bear L to
e exit near the A323 (150m).

Cross the footbridges and track
d follow the edge of the wood
R (paths inside or outside the
es) to the top corner (600m). ✪

Extension of 2.2 km/1⅓ mile:
llow the vehicle track to the road
00m). Opposite, take the path
ead (30m) then bear R on the
lique path. Stay ahead through
e trees, avoiding all L turns, ever
wards, to the top corner of the
ass near a house (900m). Cross
e drive and go on under trees to
e next drive (near pond) (250m).

Turn R to the Pinks Hill unmade
ad (50m). Cross slightly L and
ke the bridleway R of the drive,
rving R (60m). Turn L then stay
the same track with many bends
a vehicle cross track (550m). ☆

Turn R along the track to Wood
treet Village *(300m).* ❀

Soon after the side road R,
ear L over the grass and the road
the top R corner of the village
reen (300m). Carry on beside the
ain road briefly (40m) then cross.

ⓘ Take the track between gardens
ot the 1st field R (100m) then follow
the path at the fence (150m). Cross
the stream and go straight up the
field to the exit under trees at the
top L corner (300m). Take the path
in the trees, down the hillside into
the field with the hillock (200m), R
to the corner (50m), on through the
trees and over the footbridge at the
bottom (300m). ✪✳ →⑩ *Turn L.*

⑧ Turn R along the top edge of
the open Common to the corner
(350m). Go into the trees and over
the footbridge to the drive 20m L of
the garden gate (50m). Out of sight
ahead is another house. Slightly L,
take the path in the trees (40m)
then zigzag RLRL to the corner of
the garden fence (70m).

⑨ Cross the footbridge and go on
L of the fence (80m). After the farm
drive carry on between fields
(700m). Continue round the edge of
the field past a footbridge L (200m).

⑩ Stay on the winding track round
the front of Littlefield Manor (200m).
Carry on along the tarmac drive ❀
past houses R & L (400m).

⑪ At the L bend (to the A323) turn
R into the Littlefield Common trees
(30m). Fork L and converge on the
main road L. The path winds and
crosses several bridges, to the
corner of a garden (500m).

⑫ Go R along the verge (50m)
then cross and follow the diverging
path opposite (50m). Continue past
the houses to the road (200m).

⑬ Turn L to Merrist Wood College
and follow the drive (use the side-
walks) up to the top (700m). ✿❖

⑭ At the T-junction, turn R and
follow the drive out to Worplesdon
opposite the *White Lyon* (750m).

4 Normandy, Wood Street Village and Flexford

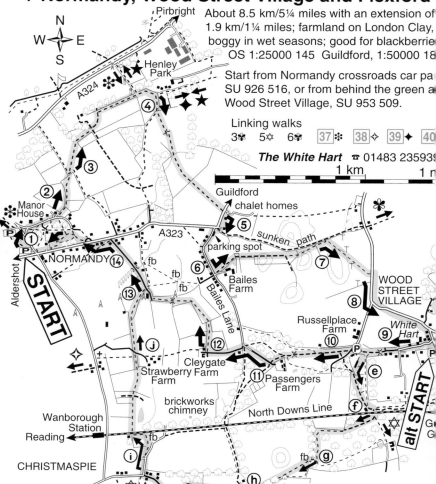

About 8.5 km/5¼ miles with an extension of 1.9 km/1¼ miles; farmland on London Clay, boggy in wet seasons; good for blackberries. OS 1:25000 145 Guildford, 1:50000 18

Start from Normandy crossroads car park SU 926 516, or from behind the green at Wood Street Village, SU 953 509.

Linking walks
3❋ 5✿ 6❋ 37❋ 38◇ 39✦ 40

The White Hart ☎ 01483 235939

❋① From the inner corner of the Normandy car park, cross two footbridges (30m) then bear R over the grass (60m) to take Normandy Common Lane past the Manor House to the R bend (250m).

② Turn L on the footpath beside the drive of Hunts Hill Farmhouse and follow the L edge of the small fields then bear R to the exit near the top R hedge corner (350m).

③ Don't go on up the edge in the large field but cross ½R towards the nearest trees (200m). Pass below the next group of trees, over a track (120m) and obliquely L up the gap in the top hedge (100m). Turn, R of the hedge, towards the Henley Park houses (300m). ✦ After a side path L (40m), the path ahead bends ½R down to the path junction below the gardens (100m)

8

④ Turn down into the boggy field 100m) then aim ½ L for the brick ridge (150m). Carry on L of the wood to the gate (400m) and over he next field to the A323 (300m).

⑤ Go R on the pavement to the end (150m) then L on Bailes Lane to the gate of Bailes Farm (400m).

⑥ Take the footpath L of the drive round to the footbridge (200m) then cross the hilltop to the gate 30m R

> Southwards is the chalk ridge of the Hogs Back. Northwards is the level profile of the Ice Age river bed of the Blackwater (terrace 8) at Ash Ranges.

of the corner (400m). Keep on to the next corner then follow the L hedge to the gate from the sunken path (200m). Don't go through it. ❀

⑦ Turn R away from the hedge on he footpath (usually invisible) over he L flank of the hill, converging on the road to the field gate (400m).

⑧ Follow the pavements R to Wood Street Village green (600m) and turn R up the edge (50m).

⑨ Take the side lane R past the **White Hart** (250m) and stay ahead to the cricket field L (250m). ✿

ⓔ *Extension of 1.9 km/1¼ miles: Cross the cricket field to the trees at the furthest corner (200m) and go L on the path outside it (250m).*

ⓕ *Pass under the railway and fork R on the path in the trees to the corner of the wood (400m). Curve L up the edge (200m).*

ⓖ *50m before the next corner take the path R, out of the wood, over a ditch (20m). The public footpath cuts straight over the field to the L edge at the large trees (250m) but walkers also go round the L edge. Stay beside the hedge down to the unmade road (250m).*

ⓗ *Turn R (400m). Keep on, round L & R bends (60m), over the rise past West Flexford Farm and down to Flexford Road in the dip (300m).*

ⓘ *Turn R down Flexford Road to the house, Little Flexford L (120m). From the drive follow the path next to the stream, past the retting pond, to the railway embankment (150m). Turn L (70m) then cross the railway lines and stay ahead along the field boundaries (600m).*

ⓙ *At Strawberry Farm cross the gravel drive and go on along the L edge of the fields (250m). Just before a house L, bear R across the field to the track beyond the barns (250m). Turn L.* ➔⑬

⑩ Carry on along the bridleway over a track, past a modern house R (300m) and round L to the drive of Passengers Farm (350m)

⑪ Turn R along the drive to the junction of tracks and paths (200m) and take the farm track L to the houses at the end (250m). ✧

⑫ Enter the R field just before the house. Go along the L hedge then between fields (250m). In the next field converge on the L hedge (200m) and turn L into the side arm of the field aiming for the middle at the end (150m). Cross the foot-bridge and keep on, bearing R of the barns to the cross path (200m).

⑬ Stay ahead on the track to the A323 (450m).

⑭ Walk along the pavement L (150m). Cross into the 2nd opening of the track opposite and take the path L (100m). After the footbridge go round the pond to the far end. Keep on along the path which bends L to the road (200m) near Normandy crossroads R (100m).

5 Wanborough, Wood Street Village & Flexford

About 7.8 km/4¾ miles; mainly farmland and woods; gentle inclines; half shady boggy in wet seasons. OS maps 1:25000 145 Guildford, 1:50000 186 Aldershot

Start at Wanborough, parking beside the Great Barn, SU 933 489. or from Woo Street Village at the top corner of the green, SU 953 509.

Linking walks 3✫ 4✪ 6✳ 7✧ ⟨2⟩✳ 24 ✳

The White Hart ☎ 01483 235939
The Royal Oak ☎ 01483 235137

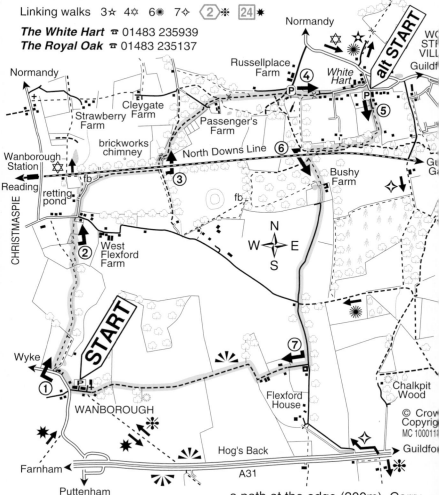

① From the road junction near Wanborough Great Barn, follow the the pavement down R, round the L curve (200m) and cross into the first field R. Go straight down. The RoW is parallel with the R hedge 50m from it but walkers also make

a path at the edge (300m). Carry on down the R edge of the second field (500m) and the third (200m). ② At the 4th field turn R across the stepping stones and carry on R of the brook to the road junction (100m). Stay ahead on Flexford Road, curving R after Little Flexford and the retting pond (400m). ✧ Just before the bridge turn R into the field and follow the L edge beside the railway (see <u>Flexford brickworks</u> chimney, L) (350m).

③ At the end, turn L under the railway. Cross the stream and go on through the wood (250m). Fork R (300m), cross Passenger's Farm drive and continue past another house L behind the trees (300m) to the cricket field R (300m)

④ Continue ahead to the village (200m), then on the gravel track and tarmac past the ***White Hart*** (300m). Bear R across the grass past the hidden pond to the top corner of the green (100m). ✳✧

⑤ From <u>Wood Street</u> Village take the track out of the car park in the belt of trees round outside the field.

The track eventually bends L to a T-junction (350m). ✦ Turn R at the T-junction but, if dry, go along the side path R just before it. Keep on to the railway bridge L (400m).

⑥ Pass under the railway (30m) and fork L through the wood to the edge near Bushy Farm (200m). Go along the drive and on up the track to the junction at the next house (800m). ✳ Stay ahead up to the drive R at Flexford Farm (400m).

⑦ Turn R on the drive and continue on the track ahead past barns and house (200m), round the R & L bends (100m) and between fields at the foot of the Hog's Back L. ⟋⟍ The distant ridge R is the Tertiary Sands escarpment. Keep on to the church and manor house R at Wanborough (1000m). ✳

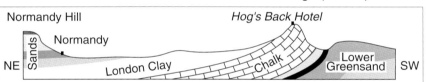

The strata on this side of the North Downs are the London Clay and the sands of the Bagshot Series of the Eocene geological period. The Chalk lies under them, dipping northwards from the ridge. Water gushes from the chalk over the top edge of the London Clay. The stream out of Wanborough would be the early cause of habitation.

The London Clay yields crocodile and palm seed fossils suggesting it formed in an estuary when the sea was hotter and/or Wanborough was closer to the equator. It underlies most of the route of the walk and is unkind to walkers in wet seasons. The soil is stodgy and easily waterlogged; farmland needs deep ditches. Often adequate only for pasture and wood, it can be fertile at its fringes next to the Chalk or Sands.

The Bagshot Series Sands are visible as the escarpment looking northwards from the Hog's Back. They form the hump of heathland occupied by Ash, Camberley, Aldershot and Chobham with the north edge at Bracknell. The heath is good for soldier-training and dog-walking but not tilling. Normandy, Henley Park and Merrist Wood are on the edge of the escarpment. The Upper, Middle & Lower Sands have been renamed Barton, Bracklesham & Bagshot Beds so *Bagshot* can mean all or part. *Tertiary Sands* covers all.

The London Clay causes clayey soil and the Tertiary Sands cause sandy soil. They are generally perceived merely as deep layers of soil, but both are geological strata up to 130m/400' thick - but unlithified.

6 Wood Street Village and Broadstreet Common

About 7.4 km/4²/₃ miles; undulating fields and the common on the London Clay; muddy in winter. OS maps 1:25000 145 Guildford, 1:50000 186 Aldershot.

Start at the car park behind the village green in Wood Street Village, SU 953 509.

Linking walks 3❂ 4✿ 5✳ 7☆ 39 ✳

The White Hart
☎ 01483 235939
The Royal Oak
☎ 01483 235137
The Cricketers
☎ 01483 575901

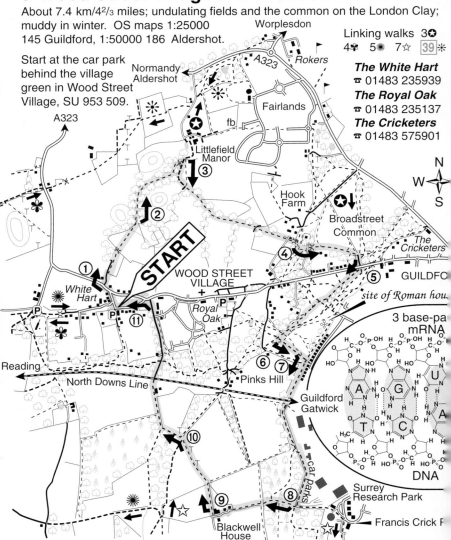

✿① At Wood Street village, walk along the broad end of the village green past **White Hart** Lane (see the iron disc L in the tarmac) to the road (150m) and L round the corner (40m). Cross the road and take the track between gardens (100m). At the first field R join the path beside the fence and continue to the end (150m). Cross the stream and go straight up the hillside, over the top, to the exit in the trees at the top L corner of the field (300m).

② Take the path in the trees down to the field with the hillock (200m). Turn R to the near corner (50m). Go on into the trees and over the footbridge at the bottom (300m).❂✳

) Turn R along the track (200m).
tay ahead on the path between
elds (700m), over the farm drive to
he fence corner & footbridge (50m).

) Out of sight ahead is a house
nd the grassland of Broadstreet
ommon. At the next path (30m)
igzag R L R L round to the tarmac
rive (80m). Outside the garden
ate 20m, take the path over the
ootbridge to the open grass (50m).
tay ahead, L of the trees, to the
ehicle track R (400m).

) Turn R to the road (100m) and
ross. Take the ½R path diverging
om the road. Keep on in the same
irection always upwards past
nany branch paths and clumps of
rees to the major cross path at the
op of the slope, in sight of a distant
himney L (RS Hospital) (700m).

) Turn L on this cross path down
o the stream near houses (250m).

7) Go R between the houses and
eld (350m), under the North
Downs Line to the end of the R
eld (300m). Keep on always at
he edge of the wood to the pond
n the trees opposite the last car
park (Research Park) (400m). ☆

8) Turn R (W) on the rising path
hough the wood to a field (250m).
Continue at the edge (250m) then
n the drive to the L bend at
Blackwell House (100m). ✳

9) Turn R on the path beside the
buildings, along R edges to the
path junction at the wood (600m).

10) Cross the bridleway, slightly R,
Continue, outside the field, over
he railway lines (500m) and on to
Wood Street Village (600m).

11) Just before the road, turn L and
make for the top L corner of the
village green and car park (300m).

The **Genetic Code** organises proteins. A protein molecule is made of amino acid molecules joined in a sequence specific to its kind. The thousands of different proteins made in cells are structural components and enzymes to promote chemical reactions. It is they which cause differences in cells and species. Other large molecules like cellulose are built from uniform small molecules with no sequence.

In a cell, an amino acid molecule grabs a specific transfer-RNA molecule that acts as a tool to fix it on a jig beside the next one. The jig is a messenger-RNA molecule composed typically of 200-600 molecules called bases: **A**denine, **U**racil, **G**uanine & **C**ytosine. Each tRNA tool has a triplet of bases which engage with three on the coded mRNA jig. They fit correctly because they pair off, A with U and G with C. These pairs are equal in length so the amino acids get lined up for linking.

amino acids *alanine* *leucine* *glycine*

tRNA "tool"
base triplet G C A C U U G A G
mRNA jig C G U G A A C C U

The master copy for this code is in the DNA of chromosomes which has base sequences for transcribing into mRNA. The bases pair off in the same way but DNA uses **T**hymine instead of **U**.

mRNA C A G U A G A G U C

DNA G T C A T C T C A G G

DNA replicates itself the same way, to pass copies to new cells and offspring.

DNA C A G G A T A G T C

DNA G T C C T A T C A G G

A gene is a unit of DNA that codes for a protein or for a switch molecule. The switches control enzymes and cause cells to take on different forms during development. This system appears improbably complex but we know it exists because artificial DNA makes the corresponding artificial proteins. Mis-copied bases cause mutations as they produce defective proteins. All organisms use the same system which is the evidence for a single ancestor.

7 Compton, the Hog's Back and Manor Farm

About 7.3 km/4½ miles. The extension of 2.0 km/1¼ mile, on the London Clay, is very muddy in wet seasons. A North Downs walk with splendid views on both sides; steep slopes. OS maps 1:25000 145 Guildford, 1:50000 186 Aldershot.

Start from Down Lane, either parking outside Watts Gallery at the bottom, in Compton, SU 957 477, or in the layby at the top, SU 967 486, near the A31.

Linking walks 3❂ 5✧ 6☆ 8❂ 18❀ ⟨2⟩★ ⟨4⟩✳ ⟨5⟩❖ 24 ✳

Watts Gallery ☎ 01483 81023
Tea Shop ☎ 01483 810232

★ ① At Compton go down the road from Watts Gallery (50m) and R on the tarmac drive (NDW) under two bridges to Monks Hatch (300m).

② Turn R on the path after the A3 bridge beside the A3 embankment (150m). After the field follow the path L through the trees and up the fields. Cross the drive 50m L of the house and continue steeply to the field gate at the top of the Hog's Back (600m).

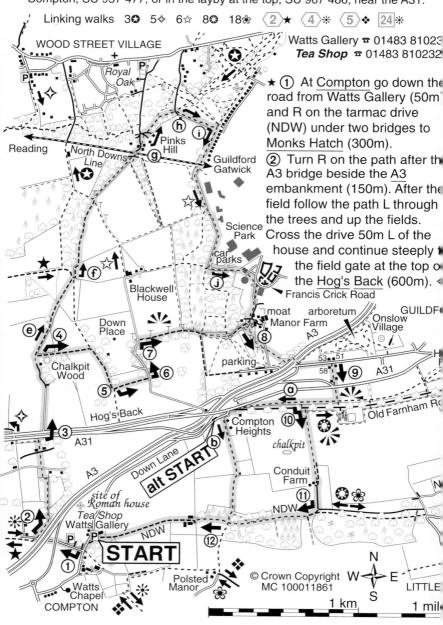

© Crown Copyright
MC 100011861

) Go R (40m) then cross the dual
arriageway. ↘ Go down the
rive to Chalkpit Cottage (500m)
nd past it to the side path R (50m).

) *Extension of 2.0 km/1¼ mile to
ink's Hill: Stay ahead down the R
dge of the field (200m), R of the
ees and across the fields (400m).*

) *Go on through a gateway and
' of the wood to side paths R & L
;00m).* ❂ *Continue ahead outside
ie field to the track (400m) then
ross the railway to the hamlet
nd* Broadstreet Common *(100m).*

) *At the second house R, bear R
ver the grass to a drive. Go along
ie branch drive (30m). Before the
ond take the path L through the
ees near the field R (300m).*

) *After the next house drive
ear R on the path along the edge
f the Common (300m).*

) *Go round the end of the field R
nd along a path in the trees R of
ouses (200m). After the railway
eep on to the end of the R field
?00m) then cross the ditch L and
ollow the edge of the wood beside
ie Science Park (400m) to the
orner at the last car park.*

) *Turn L up the edge of the wood
150m) and curve R down to the
urving road (100m). Immediately
ear R on the path L of the little
ide road (100m). Continue R of
ie* Manor Farm *track (120m) and
head into the field (40m).* ➔⑧

) Follow the path R between the
eld and Chalkpit Wood (350m)
hen up R outside the field (300m).

) Turn L with the track across the
eld to the tarmac drive (250m).

) Walk down the drive L (200m).
ork R (100m), instead of
ontinuing to Down Place. ☆

⑦ Take the track R in the next field
to the wood (300m) and down
beside it (130m). At the R bend
enter the L field. Follow the top
edge round L and down (150m).
After the clump of trees (clay pit) R
(100m), diverge on the side path R.

⑧ Make for halfway up the rising
L edge (120m). After the garden
corner (60m) take the path L over
the lane (30m). Diverge ½L from
the lane up to the high footbridge
(150m). Cross the A3 (80m) and
walk along Manor Way (250m).

⑨ At No 58, turn R up between
gardens (100m). Cross the A31 and
go straight up the field (100m). ↘

> The City of London is R of the slight
> rise behind the cathedral. W London
> is L of the rise with Terminal 5 beyond
> Woking. Bagshot Heath rises ½ L.

Turn R along the top of the field to
the first gate L (250m). ✻❂

ⓐ *Equal alternative: Stay ahead
in the field (450m). Just before the
end, cut through the trees L to the
track. Turn R to the road (50m)
and L round the verge (100m).*

ⓑ *At the corner of the Compton
Heights wall go down the footpath
beside fields, eventually rising
through the trees to a cross path,
NDW (700m).* ✻❖ *Turn R.* ➔⑫

⑩ Exit L to the Old Farnham Road,
a track (20m). Turn L (40m) then R
on the side path. ↘ Drop down

> Distant hills: Leith ½L,11 km/6¾m >
> Hascombe ahead, flat top, 9½ km/6m
> > Blackdown asymmetric, 20 km/12m
> > Gibbet ½R lumpy, 20 km/14½m.

the chalk escarpment, L of Conduit
Farm, to the track junction (700m).

⑪ Turn R along the sandy NDW
to the next cross path (600m).

⑫ Continue on bridleway then
track to Watts Gallery (1000m).

8 Guildford, the River Wey and Hog's Back

About 7.7 km/4¾ miles, with an extension of 850m/½ mile and 1.3 km/¾ mile; mostly level but with two short steep rises, splendid views, good in winter. The Wey floods but rarely. OS maps 1:25000 145 Guildford, 1:50000 186 Aldershot.

On foot, join from Guildford or bus and railway stations. Millmead car park is free on Sundays, SU 994 492. On the extension, there is free parking at the layby near the top of Down Lane on the Hog's Back SU 967 486.

The White House ☎ 01483 302006   **The Britannia** ☎ 01483 572160
The Weyside ☎ 01483 568024   **Ye Olde Ship** ☎ 01483 575731

Linking walks 7◐ 9✜ 18✿ 19✸ 20✳ 25✦ ⟨8⟩✛   A31 Hog's Back

Farnham ◄   A3   Compton ◢ **alt START**

① From Millmead car park, cross the river to Millmead Lock (50m). ✳ Turn R along the lock and keep on at the water's edge (300m).

② Soon after the **Weyside**, cross the river footbridge L. Turn R over the rowing club drive (40m). After it (25m), diverge R on the meadow path ✦✛ to the far end of the distant wood (750m). Turn L beside the Navigation to the footbridge (200m). Cross to the towpath. ✿

ⓔ *Extension of 850m/½ mile: Go L on the towpath (300m), past the confluence with the* River Wey, *to St Catherine's Lock (350m).*

ⓕ *Turn R on the track under the railway to the A3100 (300m).*

ⓖ *Cross. Go L on the pavement (100m) and R up The Ridges (170m). At the bend stay ahead up the path to Littleton (900m).*

ⓗ *Walk up the road R to the bend (350m), ahead on the drive (50m), L on the North Downs Way.* ✦⑤

③ Turn R (40m) then L up the foot path beside the spring. Keep on up Ferry Lane over the railway to the A3100, opposite the drive of Brabœuf Manor (University of Law) (200m). (St Catherine's Hill back L with chapel) (100m). Go R on the pavement down to **Ye Olde Ship** (50m) then cross the road.

④ Go along Sandy Lane (200m). Turn R on the North Downs Way track (800m). Stay ahead up the farm drive (400m) and round the L bend on top (100m). ✿ Turn R with the NDW.

⑤ Carry on up (300m) and down to the next track junction (400m).

ⓧ *Extension of 1.3 km/¾ mile: Stay on the NDW over the rise to the next cross path (650m).* ❸

ⓨ *Turn R down off the Greensand and continue up the path on the Chalk to the A31 (750m).*

ⓩ *From the top of Down Lane go R along the A31 verge. After the the track (Old Farnham Road) (30m), turn into the field. Follow the edge to the first gate R (450m). Outside the field, turn L on the track (OFR) (40m), R on the next side path (30m) and L into the field.* ✦⑦

⑥ Go up the track R past Conduit Farm then up the path (700m). Just before the top turn into the R field.

⑦ Follow the permissive path ↘ along the top edge (200m), around the masts (350m) and on (450m).

⑧ Just before the next hedge turn L across the Old Farnham Road to the field on the N side. Carry on

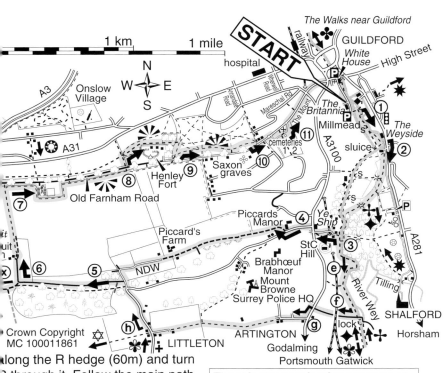

The Walks near Guildford

along the R hedge (60m) and turn
R through it. Follow the main path
past the Henley Fort houses R and
through the trees (350m). Turn R
into the corner to see the memorial
for the Cornish Rebellion (100m).
⑨ Go back to the brow and along
the field ↘↗ eventually into the R
corner near the houses (600m).
⑩ Turn L down the road (100m),
R into the cemetery (25m), L on the
tarmac side path (50m), to the 2nd
cemetery. Go down to the grave of
Lewis Carroll R (white cross) (50m).
⑪ Go past the chapel, to the road,
and descend (in line with Guildford
High Street) (500m). Cross the
A3100 and go on past St Nicholas
Church (see flood mark) (100m). ♣
Between Town Bridge and the
White House, drop to the water's
edge and follow the Godalming
Navigation to Millmead car park
and the **Britannia** (300m).

The **telecommunications towers** at
the E end of the Hog's Back are visible
for many miles around. They share
the site with a Guildford reservoir of
2,200m³/½m gallons. The tallest mast,
45m high, was built for the BBC in the
1970s but is now used by all the TV
companies. The glass fibre cylinder on
top protects antennæ for analogue
signals that were beamed downwards
to limit the range to 10 miles. The
square ærials are for digital TV and
radio. The vertical bar ærials are for
mobile phones. The mast with many
dish ærials is for government signals:
defence, police, ambulances, etc.
The one with small antennæ belongs
to Thames Water and is for voice links
to vehicles, admin data transmission,
and signals to and from unmanned
installations such as height gauges,
flow meters, pumps and valves. The
mobile-phone tower has vertical bar
ærials facing three ways. Other users
rent space on the masts for antennæ.

17

9 Stoke-juxta-Guildford and Riverside Park

About 6.8 km/4¼ miles; a Wey Navigation walk mainly flat, with a short cut of 1 km/¾ mile. A short section through the streets of Guildford is required to make the route circular. The walk is best when Dapdune Wharf Navigation Centre is open (11-5, Thurs-Mon Apr-Oct). OS 1:25000 145 Guildford; 1:50000 186 Aldershot.

Start from Guildford College car park, SU 997 504 (public & free at weekends & holidays), or Woodbridge retail centre (2-hour), SU 991 508, or the E car park at Spectrum, TQ 007 510.

The Rowbarge ☎ 01483 570242
The King's Head ☎ 01483 568957
The Stoke Pub ☎ 01483 504296
Wey Navigations ☎ 01483 561389

Linking walks: 8✣ 10✲

(map of Stoke-juxta-Guildford and Riverside Park with labels: Jacobswell, weir, Slyfield Industrial Estate, Woking, Stoke, Stoke Lock, Burp, Riverside Park, Row Barge, Stoke Mill, Spectrum, Navigation, River Wey, Waterloo, Woking, alt START, Aldershot, Hog's Back, Farnborough, Reading, railway, A320, A3, A25, A322, A246, START, Guildford College, Stoke Park, Water, Leatherh, Great Book, Effingham Jun, East Horsley, West Clandon, The Stoke, Dapdune Wharf, cathedral, GUILDFORD, King's Head, Stoke Hospital, Prince Albert, Guildford Town Centre, Leatherhead, Dorking, Hog's Back, A31, High Street, A3100, A281, Godalming, Horsham, © Crown Copyright MC 100011861, 1 mile scale, N W E S compass)

of the *Prince Albert*, between gardens. Zigzag ahead to the play area then cross R to Drummond Road (150m). Turn L to the main road (200m) and cross ½R towards Guildford Cricket Ground (50m).

ⓘ If Dapdune is closed make for the railway bridge and take the footpath L of the embankment. ➔④

Leave the Guildford College car park at the corner furthest from the road and buildings and bear R

① Take the straight path along Stoke Park Gardens to the road (100m). Go down under the railway (60m) and along Stoke Road past the *Stoke* and *Kings Head* (150m).

② Opposite the end of the Stoke Hospital L, take the passageway, R

③ Walk along Wharf Road (100m) then R on the drive to Dapdune Wharf (100m). In the car park go L to the wharf then return (100m) and go on along the cricket ground hedge. At the end turn L & R to the gateway next to the railway (200m).

④ Cross the footbridge and drop to the Wey Navigation (100m), ✤ Follow the towpath, R of the road (350m). Just before the road bridge ascend L. Cross the dual carriageway then cross the bridge (50m).

⑤ Join the towpath outside the retail car park. Pass under the A3, round a R bend and opposite the *Rowbarge* to the split of the River Wey and Navigation (1000m). Ascend to the road and cross to the drive of Stoke Mill (100m). Step in to see the turbine R, then go over the river bridge (50m). (For the *Rowbarge*, cross the Navigation bridge then the road (200m).)

⑥ Before the Navigation bridge rejoin the towpath R and stay on it to Stoke Lock (600m). ✤

⑦ Cross the footbridge R (50m). Turn L along the towpath (100m) and R along the boardwalk (70m). Cross another path then aim for the pond in Riverside Park (80m).

⑧ Halfway across the wide end turn R over the grass; aim R of the distant Leisure Centre building, over the rise, to the river (400m). Continue along the river bank and under the A3 bridge (300m).

ⓢ *Short cut of 1 km/¾ mile: Stay beside the river (80m) and continue on the path up through dragons' teeth and trees to the road (150m).*

ⓣ *Cross. Go round the trees to the grass of Stoke Park (100m) and up the middle of the knoll (200m).* ➔⑪

⑨ Turn L up beside the A3 (250m). Keep to the same path in the trees past a wide cross path (200m) to the fork (250m) then R to the A25 (150m). Cross to Stoke Park.

⑩ Turn R then diverge from the road. L of the trees, make for the middle of the distant knoll (750m).

⑪ From the top, aim for the gate of Stoke Park Gardens ie towards Guildford Cathedral and the bottom end of the line of trees L (200m). Go down past the L end of the pond and ahead through the rock garden to the L corner of the College car park (150m). To continue, go L. ➔①

Alan Turing's family lived near Stoke Park from 1927 when he was 15. He became a mathematician, renowned for breaking the German Enigma cyphers and devising the computer.

At Kings College Cambridge in 1935 he had the idea of a machine which could follow rules for standard calculations and would be universal IF it used a store of procedures. He could see no limit to artificial intelligence.

He was interested in cypher-theory before the Second World War and was recruited for the code-breaking centre at Bletchley Park. He helped develop the *bombes*, machines using punched tape to test thousands of possible decrypts. A telephone engineer, Tommy Flowers, made electronic components for the bombes and eventually built Colossus, an all-electric replacement.

Turing taught himself electronics to participate. After the war he went to Manchester University where the first programmable computer ran 21/6/48. He liaised with the USA about code breaking during the war and about building computers after the war.

He became an FRS in 1951 and was prosecuted for gross indecency in 1952. Faced with a year in prison or a year's injections to cure his homosexuality, he chose "cure". In 1954 he killed himself, reasons unknown. He would be seen as a great security risk.

When he died, the code-breaking was still secret so he never received public recognition for his war work. He was investigating plant development when Crick published the structure of DNA (1953) and foresaw the genetic code.

Alan Turin the Enigma A Hodges 2014 736p

10 Jacobswell and the Wey Navigation

About 9.6 km/6 miles; almost flat, along a tranquil part of the Wey Navigation with an unpleasant ½ mile through Slyfield Industrial Estate to make the route circular. OS maps 1:25000 145 Guildford, 1:50000 186 Aldershot.

In the week start from Jacobswell village hall, TQ 000 530 or Riverside Park, TQ 011 526 or St Edward the Confessor Church, TQ 005 538. At weekends there is lots of parking in the Slyfield Industrial Estate, TQ 005 523.

Linking walks   9✳   11✡   15 ✳

The Olive Tree ☎ 01483 729999

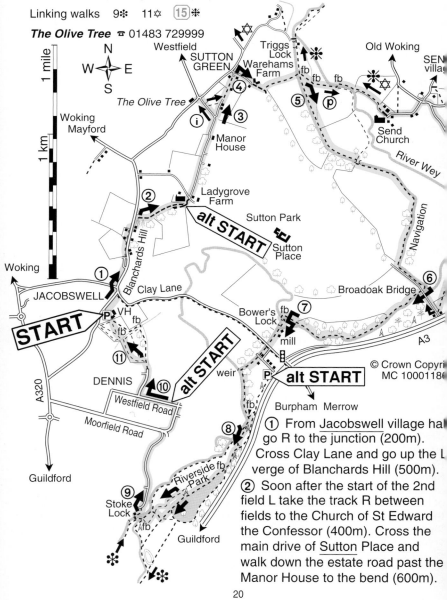

① From Jacobswell village hall go R to the junction (200m). Cross Clay Lane and go up the L verge of Blanchards Hill (500m).

② Soon after the start of the 2nd field L take the track R between fields to the Church of St Edward the Confessor (400m). Cross the main drive of Sutton Place and walk down the estate road past the Manor House to the bend (600m).

20

ⓘ *If visiting the* **Olive Tree** *(300m) to L to the main road then return, and cut L across the field obliquely.*

③ Continue on the drive ahead past houses R then along the footpath (350m). ✿

④ Turn R along Warehams Farm drive (150m) and continue on the track (100m). When it bends to the R field. bear L on the sunken path to the Wey Navigation. Cross the cart bridge (200m). Triggs Lock is visible 200m L along the canal. ❈

ⓟ *It is possible to go on over the fields to* Send Church *(800m) then along the lanes (1000m) and back over fields to the Wey near the gates of Sutton Park (600m).* ➔⑥

⑤ Turn R along the towpath to Send Church Bridge (700m) and continue on the other side to Broadoak Bridge at the weir where the River Wey and Navigation split (see roller for tow ropes) (1200m).

⑥ Go under Broadoak Bridge and continue to Bower's Lock (950m).

⑦ Cross the river and lock (50m) and go on along the towpath over the mill race, under a high road bridge and past the end of a road with houses (car park at far end) (300m). Keep on past the river weir (150m) and the R curve with a low footbridge L (350m) to the next side path (on the board walk) (80m). ❈

⑧ Take this side path to Riverside Park, over a little rise and halfway along R of the pond (650m). Either turn R onto the boardwalk and follow it to the end (400m) or stay ahead (150m) and, after the pond (50m), turn R along the boardwalk (60m) and L to the bridge (100m).

⑨ Cross the river footbridge and Stoke Lock footbridge (where river & Navigation meet). Turn R at the water's edge past the cottage and up to the lane (60m). Follow the lane R to the Slyfield Industrial Estate (600m). Stay ahead L of Moorfield Road (200m).

⑩ Turn L along Westfield Road (250m) and R along North Moors Road (250m). Continue briefly on the path into the trees (30m).

⑪ Fork L into the field. Go round the L edge and down over the ditch to the next field (250m). Look for the village hall at the top edge and make for it obliquely R (150m).

Sutton Place cannot be seen from any public place. It was built in the 1520s for Sir Richard Weston, a diplomat of Henry VIII and was the first large house without moat and crenellation. Originally a gatehouse enclosed the court-yard making it like a small Hampton Court. Later remodelling accounts for the anachronistic symmetry. Paul Getty III owned it.   *photo - author*

11 Send, Trigg's Lock and Woking Mill

About 9.6 km/6 miles with a short cut of 2.6 km/1½ miles missing Woking Mill; a flat Wey Navigation walk on Broadmead meadow paths and towpath; swampy in wet seasons. OS maps 1:25000 145 Guildford, 1:50000 186 Aldershot.

Start from Cartbridge; park at the kerbside in Potters Lane near the *New Inn*, TQ 018 560. In Old Woking there is walkers' parking at the mill. At weekends there is lots of parking opposite the mill drive. The only large parking place is not on the route: the car park at the roundabout in Old Woking, TQ 019 569.

Linking walks   10✿   16❀   17✿   ***The New Inn*** ☎ 01483 762736
                                            The Crown & Anchor ☎ 01483 766274

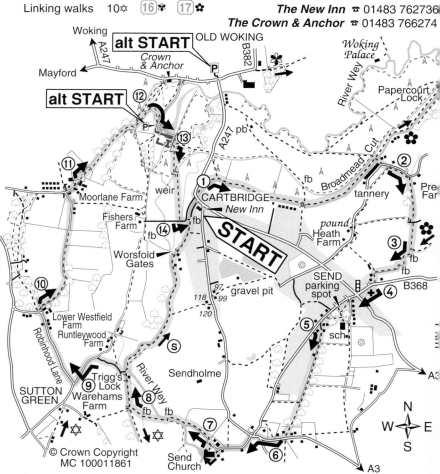

© Crown Copyright
MC 100011861

① From the ***New Inn*** cross the road bridge and drop to the towpath. Follow the Wey Navigation past the 1st footbridge (800m) to the 2nd at the end of Send Tannery, a very long building (600m). ✿

② Cross the Navigation to the road (50m). Stay ahead. Watch out for the path R (50m) and follow it R of the hedge to the stream at the bend in the lane (150m). Turn R beside the stream (300m). After the

22

pond cross the cart bridge L and carry on L of the stream (250m).

③ At the corner of the field cross the footbridge R. Keep on along the edge to the houses at Send (400m) and turn L to the road (50m).

④ Go R (150m), over Send crossroads and up the slope (250m).

⑤ After the trees turn L into the drive of Aurum and carry on along the footpath in the belt of trees to the next road (800m).

⑥ Follow the road R to staggered crossroads (300m) and turn L down the lane to Send Church (350m).

⑦ Go round the church and out at the next gate R (100m). Turn L on the path outside the garden. Stay ahead beside fields, over the Wey footbridge (500m) and R along the bank (100m). When the river bends R, stay ahead to the visible bridge at the invisible Wey Navigation, but aim L of the direct line to cross a low bridge at a ditch (200m). ✿

⑧ Go R on the towpath to Trigg's Lock (250m) (firemark on house).

Ⓢ *Short cut of 2.6 km/1½ miles missing Old Woking: keep to the towpath over the river and past the* Worsfold Gates *(900m) to the New Inn at* Cartbridge *(400m).*

⑨ Cross the Navigation L. Follow the track (200m) then the lane L from Runtley Wood Farm (200m). Turn R along Robinhood Lane to the L bend at the wood (500m).

⑩ Just round the bend (10m) turn R on the path and immediately R again into the farmyard (30m). From it enter the field L. Follow the tree-lined R edge (200m) and stay ahead along L edges (400m). Continue on the farm road and lane past houses to a T-junction (250m).

⑪ Turn R into Moorlane Farm (50m). Fork L of the barn and stay ahead on the path L of the cowshed (100m). Pass R of the ditch through the corner of the next field then follow the L edge of the field near the ditch to the narrow end (400m). Cross the bridge into the next field then follow the R edge (150m). ✿

⑫ Keep to the R edge curving in a semicircle to the trees R (200m). Cross the footbridge to the drive of Gresham (Woking) Mill (50m). Walk to the far end of the apartments (150m), round the corner (50m) and out L to Broadmead meadows.

⑬ Turn R along the edge. After the ditch follow the main path diverging slightly L, halfway between pylons, to the footbridge (250m). Cross and keep on to the farm drive (300m).

⑭ Go L over the cartbridge (50m), R over the footbridge (50m), and L on the track to the *New Inn* (200m).

Old **Woking** is WOCHINGES in the Domesday Book, a large royal manor with a mill and church. Granted away by King John, it reverted to the crown through inheritance. The palace that grew out of the manor house became a favourite residence of Henry VIII, as indicated by the many letters he sent from there. It is said Wolsey heard of his elevation to cardinal while visiting. The palace has gone but a grey outbuilding still stands and can be seen across the Broadmead from the Wey Navigation. The church was founded around 675. New Woking came about through an Act of Parliament of 1852 enabling the Necropolis Company to buy 2600 acres of Woking Common for the cemetery at Brookwood. The company sold most of the land as haphazard building plots enabling the railway station to acquire a haphazard town, 1½ miles from the church.
A History of Woking A Crosby 1982 Phillimore

12 Merrow & Pewley Downs and St Martha's Hill

About 7.6 km/4¾ miles with an extension of 2.4 km/1½ miles to Newlands Corner. A North Downs walk with fine views on both sides; hilly; the wood is very confusing. Walkers and golfers have equal rights-of-way on Merrow Downs but beware! OS maps 1:25000 145 Guildford, 1:50000 186 Aldershot.

Start: Merrow Downs car park, TQ 022 499, next to Guildford Golf Club car park or Halfpenny Lane car park, TQ 022 484. or, on the extension, Newlands Corner

Linking walks 13★ 20✻ 21❋ 22☆ 26✦ ⑩ ✿

The Horse & Groom
☎ 01438 575375
Newlands Corner Snack Bar

① Follow the uphill track from the golf club car park (100m). Go round the L bend, through trees and across the valley (300m).

② At the wood take the side track L. From the R bend, go up the edge of the trees and round R to the lumpy ground with chalk pits (200m). Keep to the edge of the wood past oblique paths R into the trees (300m). One side path, on the narrow part of the ridge, starts as a groove and goes straight down.

ⓔ *Extension of 2.4 km/1½ mile: Disregard this path R and bear L over the golf course (no path) down to the junction of the two gravel tracks at Trodd's Lane (500m). ★*

ⓕ *Cross and walk on the grass up the R edge of the golf course (500m).*

ⓖ *Before the trig point 80m take the path R under the trees (130m), over the lane and ahead to the cross path (100m).*

ⓗ *Turn L to the next cross path (150m) and L again (200m). Curve R through the yew grove (100m) and follow paths ahead straight up the slope to Newlands Corner car park (450m).* ✻☆ ↘

ⓘ *Walk along the car park (250m).*

ⓙ *Just before the end, go L on the cross path to the yew wood (70m) then R along the brow and out to open grassland (100m). Follow the edge round R (500m). Near the end fork L down through the trees to Whites Lane (200m).* ✦④

③ Take the side path R down into Walnut Tree Bottom (150m) and go straight up the other side, L of the broken wall of Keeper's Cottage

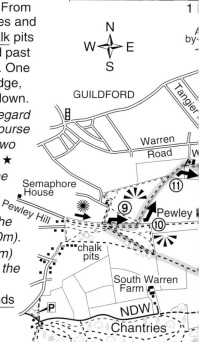

(500m). Cross the horse track and continue into White Lane car park (60m). Take the downhill path (90m) then drop R to the road (50m).

④ Cross to the path (NDW) behind the trees and walk down L to the L bend in the road (400m). ✦

ⓐ *Alternative: Go R along the track all the way to Halfpenny Lane passing through Tyting farm at the*

24

end (1200m). Keep on over the road down the track to the crossing path (400m). Turn R. →⑧

⑤ Go up the drive L of the house (North Downs Way) and ahead to the end of the path (300m).

⑥ Turn R on the wide sandy path up the edge of the hill (400m). ✪ Go through St Martha's churchyard

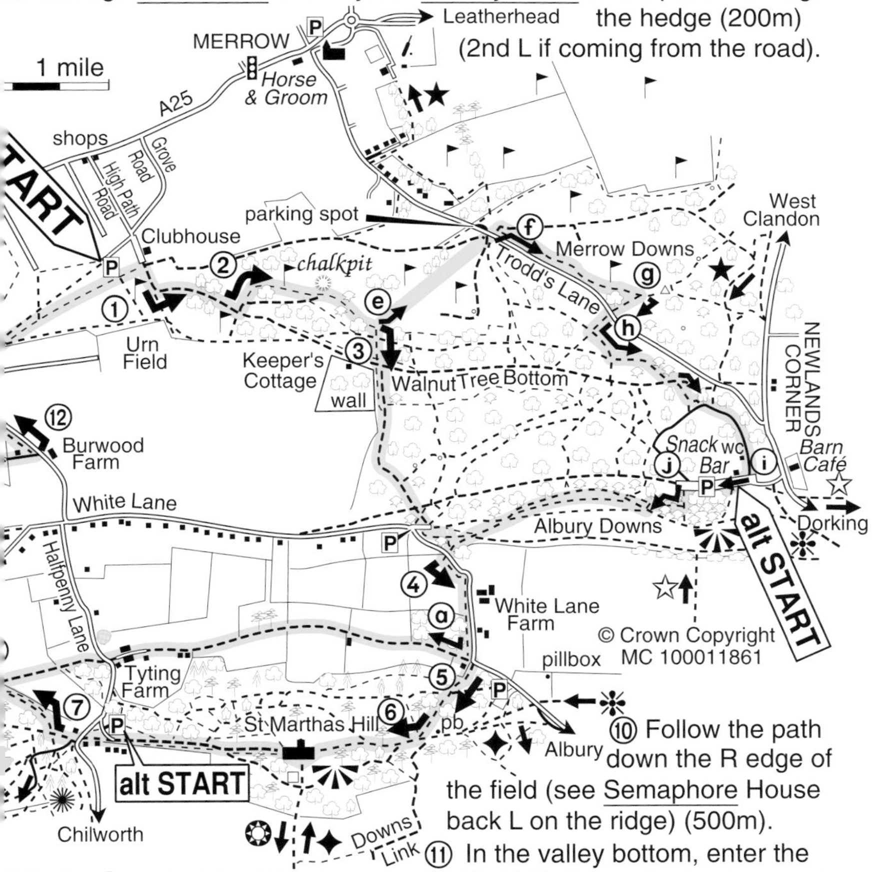

⑧ Keep on between hedges to the junction in the trees with a steep uphill path R and a diverging path L (700m). Go on (10m) then cross L to the parallel path and keep on obliquely up the hillside, L of hedge with a view L (300m). ↘

⑨ Walk back R along the top of Pewley Down to the path L through the hedge (200m) (2nd L if coming from the road).

Map labels: 1 mile · MERROW · Horse & Groom · A25 · shops · Grove Road · High Path Road · START · Clubhouse · parking spot · chalkpit · Urn Field · Keeper's Cottage · wall · Walnut Tree Bottom · Leatherhead · West Clandon · Merrow Downs · Trodd's Lane · NEWLANDS CORNER · Snack wc Bar · Barn Café · Dorking · Albury Downs · alt START · White Lane · Burwood Farm · Halfpenny Lane · White Lane Farm · © Crown Copyright MC 100011861 · pillbox · Tyting Farm · St Marthas Hill · alt START · Chilworth · Albury · Downs Link

(80m), ↘ out at the W gate and down the main track. Stay ahead past the houses L and car park R to Halfpenny Lane (700m). ☀

⑦ Go L down to the bend (30m) and R on the path beside the garden (100m). Descend the 1st R and cross the bottom track (300m).

⑩ Follow the path down the R edge of the field (see Semaphore House back L on the ridge) (500m).

⑪ In the valley bottom, enter the last field R. Go up the L edge, past Warren Farm L, and on from field to field to the next road (600m).

⑫ Walk along the verge L to the T-junction (300m).

⑬ Cross into the track opposite and turn R down one of the paths towards the golf club (650m).

13 Newlands Corner, Merrow and West Clandon

About 8 km/5 miles, with an extension of 2.7 km/1²/₃ miles; long but gentle rises; fine views on both sides of the Downs. At the time of printing, the fire-damaged Clandon House (NT) cannot be visited and the circuit through the garden may become impossible. OS maps 1:25000 145 Guildford, 1:50000 186 Aldershot.

Start at Newlands Corner car park, TQ 043 492, or at Clandon Park car park, TQ 043 513. On the extension, park in Merrow Common Road, TQ 027 517.

Linking walks
  12★ 14✹ 15❂ 21✳ 22☆
    Effinham Junction

The Bull's Head ☎ 01483 222444
The Horse & Groom ☎ 01483 575375
Newlands Corner Snack Bar

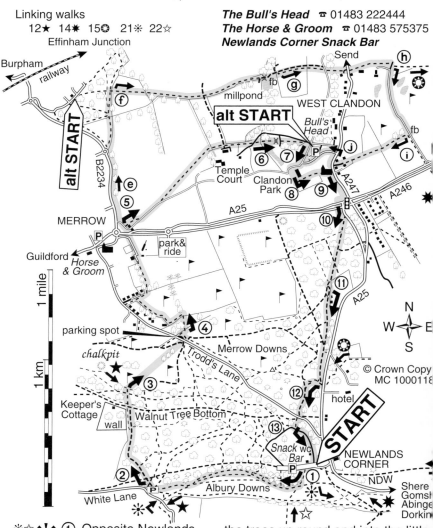

✳☆↘↙ ① Opposite Newlands Corner snack bar go down the hillside and pass round the edge of the wood R. Follow the edge of

the trees up round and into the little car park at White Lane (900m). ★
② There are three side paths R. Take the middle one, a bridleway,

26

over the main track (70m) and on through the scrub. On the descent, use the path L next to the wall (Keeper's Cottage) down to Walnut Tree Bottom (500m). Go up the other side to the golf course (200m). Walkers and golfers have equal rights-of-way on Merrow Down.

③ Aim ½R over the golf course (no path) towards the bottom R corner then make for the junction of gravel tracks at the road (600m).

④ Cross the road but don't go on along the track opposite. Take the path down the bottom edge of the golf course (80m) then L through the trees (100m). At the golf course turn L (Merrow church spire below). Follow the edge round three sides until past an obvious row of houses (450m) then bear L through the trees and follow the edge down to the tennis club (250m). Keep on down the drive to the L bend (200m). From there, cross the A25 to the ornamental gates (40m).

ⓔ *Extension of 2.7 km/1⅔ miles: Stay ahead beside Park Lane to the next roundabout (500m) then bear R along the edge of the field (250m). Continue at the R edge of the wood to the T-junction (150m).*

ⓕ *Turn R across the field (250m). Go on along the R edge into a dip with track (400m), over a rise and down to the millpond R (900m).*

ⓖ *After the footbridge take the path R of the track up to the tarmac drive (400m). Go on through the trees (100m), over the road and down the footpath to the path/drive junction in the golf course (300m).*

ⓗ *Walk along the drive R (500m).*

ⓘ *At the line of trees R, turn up the path beside the field (600m).*

ⓙ *Walk along the road R (100m) and down the drive to Clandon Park (house) (300m).* ➜⑧

⑤ Enter Clandon Park L of the L lodge. Follow the drive to the slight bend (300m) then diverge L on the path over the field and skirt the farmyard fence (550m). Stay ahead over the farm track from Temple Court R and down, outside the field, to the track from the house (200m).

⑥ Enter the field opposite. Cross the L corner to the wood (50m). Follow the footpath over the pond (300m) and carry on on the track to the tarmac drive (40m). (*If visiting the **Bull's Head** stay ahead up to the road (200m) and turn L (100m). Return via the path in the trees behind the pub garden. If not:*

⑦ Follow the tarmac drive R to Clandon Park (house)(200m).

⑧ Cross the terrace in front of the house. In the garden turn L and follow the path to West Clandon Church and the road (300m). ◉✶

⑨ Walk along the pavement R to the dual carriageway (250m) & R.

⑩ Cross at the traffic lights. Go up the R arm of Shere Road (50m) and bear R on the footpath, soon rising through a beech plantation (400m).

⑪ Soon after the corner of the field branch L towards the house (150m). Keep on up the bridleway, past a drive visible over the A25 (250m), until it L bends to the road (350m).

⑫ Before reaching the road turn R on the path crossing from the road (80m) and take the first L soon joining another path. Keep on L to the next road (250m).

⑬ Cross and ascend to the hard path (50m). Follow it up L to Newlands Corner car park (300m).

14 West Clandon and the Netherlands

About 8.3 km/5¼ miles; a hilly North Downs walk with fine views on both sides; good in winter. The woodland near Newlands Corner is confusing At the time of printing, the fire-damaged Clandon House (NT) cannot be visited and the circuit through the garden may become impossible. Two short cuts of 2.6 km/1⅔ miles or 4.2 km/2½ miles are possible only if starting from West Clandon.
OS maps 1:25000 145 Guildford, 1:50000 186 Aldershot +187 Dorking.

Start from Newlands Corner car park, TQ 043 492, or from Clandon Park car park (NT), TQ 043 513.

Linking walks
13✳ 15✿ 16✳ 21✪ 22❀ 23✿

The Bull's Head ☎ 01483 222444
Newlands Corner Snack Bar

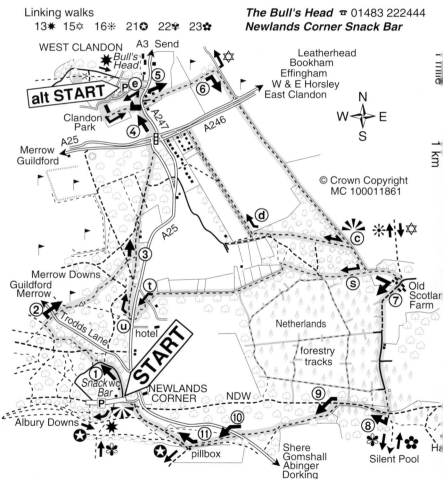

✳① From Newlands Corner car park ↘↙ take the hard path past the wc block down to the L bend (300m) then the side path ahead down to the T-junction (100m).

Slightly L take the onward path through the yew grove (100m) to the cross path (200m). Turn R and watch out for a less obvious cross path (100m).

② Turn R to Trodds Lane (100m) Cross and go through the trees to the <u>Merrow Down</u> golf course and the trig point (200m). Behind the trig point take the L path down through the wood over two cross paths to a T-junction (500m). Turn L.

③ Keep on (200m). After the farm join another path but continue in the same direction past the corner of the field (50m), down through the beechwood to the road (500m).

④ Cross the dual carriageway at the junction and take the side road to West <u>Clandon</u> Church L (350m).

ⓔ *Extension of 800m to <u>Clandon</u> Park: Go on along the road (100m) then L down the drive past the car park (300m). Cross the front of the house then go back though the garden to church and road (400m).*

⑤ Cross the road at the bend into the drive between the houses and carry on between fields (600m). ✿

⑥ At the end turn R beside the golf course drive (250m). Cross the dual carriageway into the field opposite. Go up the L edge, ⤢ through the trees on top (1300) and down to the bridleway (200m). ➜ⓒ or ➜ⓢ or ➜⑦

ⓒ *Short cut of 4.2 km/2½ miles: On the top of the hill, before the bridleway, turn R along the grass corridor between the trees (700m).*

ⓓ *Go R, down beside the hedges all the way to the A246 (900m). ➜⑤*

ⓢ *Short cut of 2.6 km/1⅔ miles: Go R on the bridleway (500m), L round the fields and on (1000m).*

ⓣ *After the last fence corner R, bear L up the winding path, over a tarmac drive to the A25 (300m).*

ⓤ *Cross into the bridleway opposite and take the R downhill branch near the road (450m). ➜④*

⑦ Walk up the bridleway L to the track at Old Scotland Farm and the brewery (200m).✳ Follow the track up R past a house L (450m) and the <u>Netherlands</u> plantations to the <u>North Downs Way</u> on the brow of the hill (450m). ✿✿

⑧ Turn R along the level NDW to a side path forking down L (300m).

⑨ Take the downhill path (500m). When it bends L continue ahead on the lesser path to the A25 (300m).

⑩ Cross to the field. Stay ahead ⤢ converging on the bottom edge and follow it to the <u>pillbox</u> (300m).✦

⑪ Ascend the sunken track R to Newlands Corner car park (400m).

Parishes on the North Downs are usually long and narrow eg Abinger is 9 x 2 miles. They run north and south from the ridge, over ground that gives them fertile land on the Chalk and poorer soils on the Clays and Sands. Rural parish boundaries usually relate to Norman manors which derive from Saxon and earlier territories.

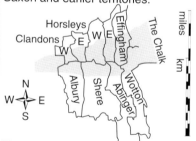

The first inhabitants would have lived on the streams issuing from the chalk above the London and Gault Clays. Presumably communities could not expand sideways because of others on adjacent streams so they spread away from the Downs. In early times the worst land on the sandy hilltops was probably Common but it would have been appended to estates when the *waste* was absorbed by farms or subdivided in the Middle Ages.

15 East & West Clandons and the North Downs

About 7.9 km/5 miles with a short cut of 850m/¾ mile; splendid views; long but gentle climbs. At the time of printing, the fire-damaged Clandon House (NT) cannot be visited and the circuit through the garden may become impossible. OS maps 1:25000 145 Guildford, 1:50000 186 Aldershot + 187 Dorking.

Start near East Clandon crossroads, on the disused Old Epsom Road just off the A246, TQ 059 515, or from Clandon Park in West Clandon, TQ 043 513.

Linking walks
13❁   14✿   16❖

The Bull's Head ☎ 01483 222444
The Queen's Head ☎ 01483 222332

© Crown Copyright
MC 100011861

❖① From Old Epsom Road at East Clandon, cross the A246 dual carriageway and start up Staples Lane (100m). Near the bend enter the R field and follow the unofficial path up beside the hedge (800m).

② Just over the brow take the public footpath ½R over the field ↘. If it is unclear, aim halfway across the top edge and 100m L of the corner of the wood (500m).

30

Follow the path in the trees to Old Scotland Farm & brewery (150m).

③ Don't join the drive. ✿ Turn back R beside the wood (200m).

Ⓢ *Short cut of 850m/¾ mile: Watch out for the footpath up R after the 1st field. Follow the fence over the top (200m) then diverge L down the grass corridor across the slope to the end (700m).*

Ⓣ *Turn R and follow the hedges straight down to the A246 (900m). Go L on the verge (150m).* ➔⑦

④ Stay on the bridleway (500m).

⑤ At the next field turn L. Keep on between wood and fields (1000m). After the last field curve L up through the trees to a drive (100m).

⑥ Turn R on the drive to the A25 (100m). Cross. Follow the little path into the trees opposite (30m) ✪ and turn R on the downhill path. Disregard the L fork (50m) and continue down L of the farm house (350m). Soon after it join another downhill path past the corner of the field (50m). Keep on down through the beech plantation and straight on to the road (500m).

⑦ Cross the dual carriageway at the junction and take the side road to West Clandon Church L (400m).

Ⓔ *NT extension to Clandon Park: Go on along the road (100m) then L down the drive past the car park (300m). Cross the front of the house then go back through the garden to the church and the road (400m).*

⑧ Cross the road at the bend to the drive between the houses and go on between fields (600m). ✿

⑨ Turn L at the end, along the golf course drive L (500m).

⑩ When the drive bends L at the end, cross the footbridge R and go

straight on over the golf course between old hedge ends (150m). Keep on in the same direction converging on the L hedge (350m). Follow the path outside the fields to the road at East Clandon (650m).

⑪ Turn L to the 3-way junction (150m); R to the T-junction (100m).

⑫ Walk R through the village, past the tithe barn to the church (200m) ❖ and R on the winding road past the **Queen's Head** towards the A246 and Old Epsom Road (250m).

The **Onslows** had their family seat at West Clandon from 1641, a family of public servants and parliamentarians. Sir Richard was first of the Salopian family to settle in Surrey, Cromwell's "Fox of Surrey" - he arrived late for the battle of Worcester and did not have to take sides. His grandson, Richard, was created Baron Onslow after being Chancellor of the Exchequer and Speaker. Arthur Onslow, 1691-1768, who lived at Levylsdene, in Merrow, was the 'Great Speaker'; he served for 33 years and initiated recording and printing proceedings. William Hillier Onslow, 4th Earl, was Governor of New Zealand 1888-1902, hence the Clandon Park Maori house. Cranley Onslow, Woking MP, but elevated to the Lords, died in 2001. The 7th Earl, who was active in the House of Lords, died in 2011.

In June, look out for scale insects on tree trunks and twigs. The most obvious species, *Pulvinaria regalis*, looks like an 8mm tortoise shell. It is most abundant on lime, horse chestnut and sycamore. It is a sap sucker in the same group as aphids but once "plugged in" the female loses its legs and just feeds and breeds. It lays its eggs in a mass of wax threads like a blob of cotton wool or mould which remains when the scale falls off.

x 1

16 East Clandon and the North Downs

About 8.4 km/5¼ miles; splendid views; slopes long but not steep. When Hatchlands Park (National Trust) is open (April-October, 12.30 - 6pm, Tu, We, Th, Su & Bank Holidays) an extension of 1 km/⅔ mile can be made though it. Dogs are not allowed and, unless you are a NT member, you should not wander in the grounds. OS maps 1:25000 145 Guildford, 1:50000 187 Dorking.

Start near East Clandon crossroads, TQ 059 515, parking on Old Epsom Road (disused) just off the A246; alternatively at West Hanger car park, TQ 070 493.

Linking 14✳ 15❖ 17✦ 22✹ 23✳ 24✣

The Queen's Head ☎ 01483 222332
Hatchlands Park NT ☎ 01483 222482

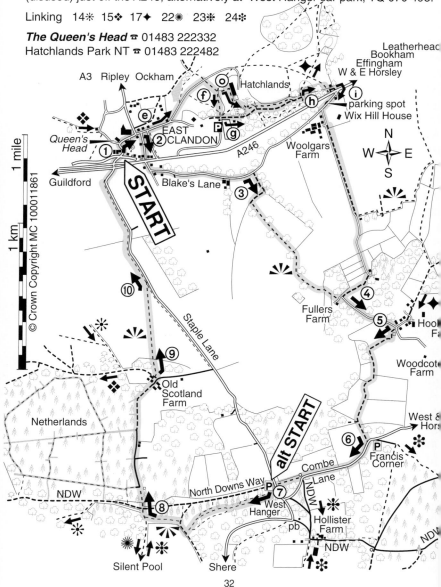

① From Old Epsom Road follow the winding road into East Clandon village past the **Queen's Head** and church (200m). Continue on the Street to School Lane R (40m).

ⓔ *Extension of 1 km/⅔ mile via Hatchlands Park. Stay ahead on the Street and Hatchlands drive to the lodge (200m). Fork L on the grass or drive up past the pond to the cross path on the very top of the rise (350m). Descend R to the gate before the house (120m).*

ⓞ If Hatchlands is open, turn L inside the gate (60m) and R along the front of the house (80m). After the little square garden, turn L over the grass into the trees. Pass L of the pit, into a dip to the icehouse. After it, turn L. Stay on this path till it bends L across the park (300m) then continue ahead in the trees on the adjacent track (80m). ➔ⓗ

ⓕ *If Hatchlands is closed, turn R outside the gate and follow the path to the end (250m). Exit to the yard with the octagonal ticket kiosk.*

ⓖ *Turn L on the track past the walled garden and keep on (600m).*

ⓗ *At the end of the track turn L out of the trees.* ✦ *Follow the park fence R over the hillock towards a house (200m). Just before it, exit R. Go along the drive past the front of the house to the A246 (50m).*

ⓘ *Cross to Blake's Lane opposite and follow it R (150m). Turn L at the first track next to Woolgar's Farm and go straight up the dip slope of the North Downs.* ⬊ *Look back over the London Basin. When the concrete track bends L to a gate (1200m), curve R on the track round the top of the fields to a tarmac drive (250m). Turn L* ➔④

② Turn R along School Lane (100m). Cross the A246 and follow Blakes Lane which soon bends L (50m). Stay on the undulating lane past farm sheds R (500m) to the next track R (200m).

③ Go up the track (150m), round R & L bends (150m) to the tarmac drive at Fullers Farm (800m). Go L up round the R bend (30m).

④ Follow the drive over the ridge and down to the houses (450m).

⑤ Turn R at the drive junction and follow the narrow winding bridleway between fields to the end at Coombe Lane (950m). ✳

⑥ Go R along the road (500m). ✳ When it bends L, stay ahead on the path and cross the next road into the car park (200m).

⑦ From West Hanger car park take the path L to the brow of the hill and follow the brow to the large slanting path beside a field (800m). ⬊ Bear R up the path (50m) then cross just above the field to the next uphill path (250m). ✳✳

⑧ Turn R and cross the NDW (40m). Continue ahead on path and track through the Netherlands pines passing a house R (450m) and curving R down to Old Scotland Farm and the brewery (500m). ❖

⑨ After the farmyard L take the uphill path through the trees into the field (150m). Continue in the same line over the top. ⬊ If the descending path is unclear, keep to the same oblique line aiming for where the hedge crosses the next brow of the slope below (500m).

⑩ Go down the unofficial path at the R edge of the field (750m). Join the road at the bottom bend. Cross the A246 to East Clandon (150m).

17 West Horsley, the Sheepleas and Wix

The main route of 8.2 km/5 miles can be used only when a gate is unlocked - April - October, 8am - 4.30pm or dusk. The gate is avoided by the extension of 1.5 km/1 mile and the short cut of 800m/½ mile; splendid views, hilly, good for winter walking. OS maps 1:25000 145 Guildford, 1:50000 187 Dorking.

Park at Sheepleas car park behind West Horsley Church car park, TQ 088 525.

Linking walks 16✦ 24✿ 38☆ 39✿ 41❄ 7 ❋

The King William IV
01483 282318
The Barley Mow
01483 282693
Hatchlands (NT)
01483 222482

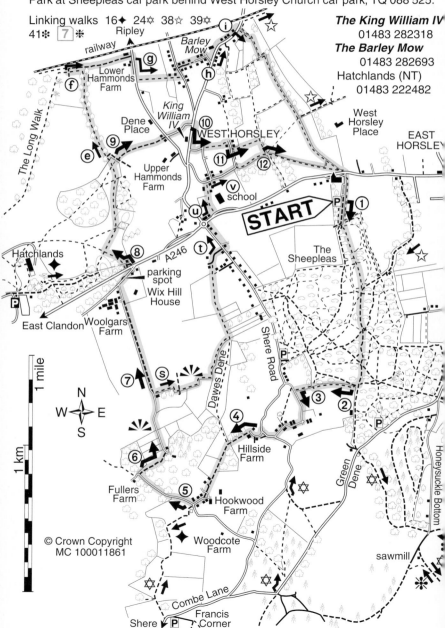

© Crown Copyright
MC 100011861

① Behind West **Horsley** Church join the track next to the field and walk away from the road (100m). At the bend stay ahead up into the Sheepleas. At each junction take the uphill path ahead to the field R on the flat top (1300m). ✿❁☆

② Walk along the R edge of the field to the farm drive (450m).

③ Go L up the farm drive to the 4-way drive junction (250m) and R past the farm buildings to the road (200m). Walk down R to the bend after the house drive L (100m).

④ Turn L up the drive of Hillside Farm (100m). On top turn L on the track past the barn. Pass between fields (450m), down a drive and up past houses to the lane (200m). ✦

⑤ Turn R up the drive over a rise and down to Fullers Farm (400m).

⑥ When the drive bends L to the house, turn R on the cart track (250m). Go round the L bend ↘↗ and on down the farm road (400m).

ⓢ *Short cut of 800m/½ mile: Near the shed R take the footpath R which winds along the edge of fields (450m). ↘↗ Eventually drop L beside a hedge and join another descending path (300m). Carry on down between fields (450m). Pass the L end of a lane with houses and keep on to the track (100m).*

ⓣ *Walk along the track R (150m) and down the road L (200m).*

ⓤ *Cross the A246 and turn R beside it (100m). Just before the school take the path L (200m).*

ⓥ *At the road, go R down to the bend (200m) and through the field along the R edge (200m). ✦⑫*

⑦ Continue ahead down past Woolgars Farm L to the lane (800m). Turn R to the A246 (150m).

⑧ Cross to the cart track opposite. Go L past the lodge (50m) then enter Hatchlands Park R. Cross the grass ½L (Hatchlands ahead) to the path from the hillock (150m). Turn R, eventually passing between two woods down to the corner (650m).

ⓔ *Extension of 1½ km/1 mile: Go straight on along the belt of trees almost to the railway (700m) then round the L bend (100m).*

ⓕ *Turn R on the track. Follow it back parallel with the railway and through the farm to the road (400m).*

ⓖ *Go up the road R (200m), L on the path over the field (300m), L on the lane (70m), R on Tintell's Lane (200m), R to the T-junction (50m).*

ⓗ *Go L on the road to the **Barley Mow** (100m) and ahead (200m). ☆*

ⓘ *After the last house L and 50m before the railway, enter the field R. Follow L edges (100m) then cross the hedge. Carry on L of it (150m), round the end of the field (30m) and on at L edges past West Horsley Place to the A246 (1200m). Cross to the church and car park (200m).*

⑨ (8am - dusk): Turn R over the park boundary and farm track. Go straight over the field, out at the lodge gates (350m) and ahead to the end of Pincott Lane (200m).

⑩ Turn R along the road past the **King William IV** (200m) then L into School Lane. Keep on along the path, which bends L round a garden to more houses (300m).

⑪ Turn R past the houses (80m), L across the field (200m) and R to the corner (100m). ☆

⑫ Enter the next field and follow the oblique path to the top corner (600m). Cross the A246 to the church and car park (200m).

18 Compton, Littleton and Loseley

About 8.0 km/5 miles with a short cut of 2.2 km/1⅓ miles; undulating Greensand with a bluebell wood. The walk may be combined with visits to Loseley House and Watts Gallery. OS maps 1:25000 145 Guildford, 1:50000 186 Aldershot.

Start from the layby opposite the *Withies*, SU 963 467, or outside Watts Gallery at Compton, SU 958 477. If visiting Loseley, start from its car park, SU 974 472.

Linking walks   7✿   8✿   19✳   ②✳   ③❂   ④❀   ⑤✳   24◆

The Withies ☎ 01483 421158   *Harrow Inn/Lemongrass* ☎ 01483 810594
Watts Gallery ☎ 01483 810235   Watts Gallery **Tea Shop** ☎ 01483 810232
Loseley House ☎ 01483 304440

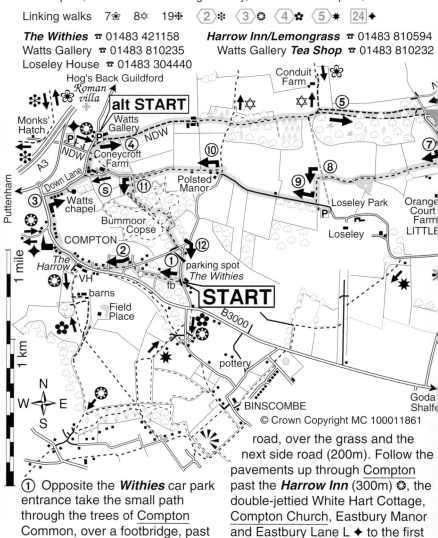

© Crown Copyright MC 100011861

① Opposite the *Withies* car park entrance take the small path through the trees of Compton Common, over a footbridge, past the frontages of two houses and round R to Polsted Lane (400m).

② Turn L to the field (50m) and cross it, converging on the main

road, over the grass and the next side road (200m). Follow the pavements up through Compton past the *Harrow Inn* (300m) ❂, the double-jettied White Hart Cottage, Compton Church, Eastbury Manor and Eastbury Lane L ◆ to the first side road R, Down Lane (550m).

③ Walk along Down Lane to the cemetery R (200m). Go up the steep cemetery path to see Watts

Chapel then carry on along the road, past Coneycroft Farm R and past the tarmac North Downs Way L (500m), to the Watts Gallery parking place (50m). ❁❁❁

④ Follow the North Downs Way, the sandy track, R of Watts Gallery, over the rise and down to the barns in the dip (750m). Carry on up the path to a 4-way junction in the trees (250m) and stay ahead to the track junction in the dip below Conduit Farm L (600m). ✡

⑤ Continue ahead up to the tarmac drive: either on the path in the trees or the sandy track, NDW, beside the field, (700m).

⑥ Turn R on the tarmac drive to the bend in the road. Continue ahead down into Littleton to the first house R (400m). ❁✳

⑦ Turn R on the track after Pillar Box Cottage. Go straight over the fields down to the pond (500m). Pass R of it and keep on to the track (400m). See Loseley far L.

⑧ Cross the track and continue on the path round the L bend (30m) to the track from Loseley (200m).

⑨ Turn R along the track to the road at Polsted Manor (700m).

⑩ Turn R up the sunken footpath in front of Little Polsted (30m) then climb out of it L on the side path beside the garden. Stay ahead at the edge of the fields (650m).

Ⓢ *Short cut of 2.2 km/1⅓ miles if parked at Watts Gallery: Go on along the concrete farm track and skirt L of the barns (450m). Follow the road R to Watts Gallery (300m).*

⑪ Approaching Coneycroft Farm cross the fence and turn L outside the fields (150m) and L into the wood. It is better to take the unofficial path L of the RoW, just before the RoW turns into the trees (200m). This bends L then R & R back to the RoW (200m). Carry on (L) to Polsted Lane (150m). ❂❀

⑫ Cross slightly L to the side road and follow it to the *Withies* (300m).

Watts Gallery is open 11-5 but not on Mondays. Close to his last home, it displays 500 works of the painter and sculptor George Watts. Art treasures from the London galleries were stored here in World War II. The adjacent buildings were a studio and factory for terracotta ware until 1956 using the underlying Gault Clay. The 1950's TV potter's wheel interlude was filmed here. A Roman house was excavated 1914 in the Watts' garden at Limnerlease yielding three coins dating from 313 to 378.

George Frederick Watts, 1817-1904, sold 5-shilling portraits at the age of 16 and served as the House Artist to the British Ambassador in Florence. His best-known work is *Physical Energy,* in Kensington Gardens. He was a friend of Dickens, Thackeray and Tennyson. His first wife was Ellen Terry.

If walking in April, look up at the oaks to see the male flowers which hang in catkins. Berry-like structures on the catkins (several kinds) are galls induced by the egg-laying of minute wasps to supply the needs of their larvæ.

19 Littleton and the Godalming Navigation

About 6.5 km/4 miles; no steep ascents; good in winter. An extension of 1.6 km/1 mile can be combined with a visit to Loseley (when open). Gentle slopes, fairly shady. OS maps 1:25000 145 Guildford, 1:50000 186 Aldershot.

Start from Shalford, parking in the side road next to *The Parrot*. SU 998 467, or from Peasmarsh, parking in the side road behind the green, SU 990 463. If visiting Loseley, the walk could start from the car park there, SU 973 472.

The Parrot ☎ 01483 561400 8✹ 18✹ 20✣ 25✤ ⟨5⟩✧ ⟨9⟩❂ ⟨10⟩☆
Ye Olde Ship ☎ 01483 575731
The Sea Horse ☎ 01483 514351
The Queen Victoria ☎ 01483 566959
Loseley Park ☎ 01483 304440

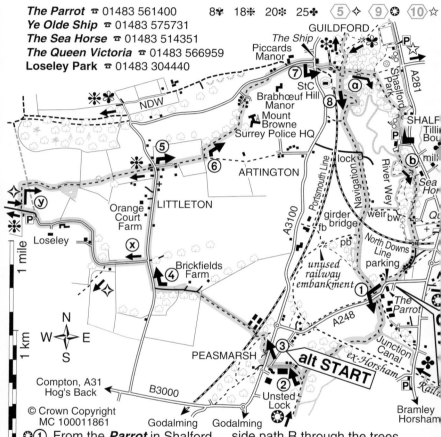

❂① From the **Parrot** in Shalford go round the bends in the A248 to the Godalming Navigation (200m). Cross the bridge and go L on the towpath, past the Junction Canal opposite (250m), under the path on the bridge of the old Horsham Railway (250m) and ahead (400m).

② Watch out ahead for Unstead Lock and, 150m before it, take the side path R through the trees. Continue on the lane to the green at Peasmarsh (300m).

③ Cross ½R: the narrow end of the green, the A3100 and the footbridge R of the pond (80m). Follow the oblique footpath through the trees to the end (150m). Go L over the railway (50m), along the R edge of the field (450m) and ahead on the drive past the pond to the road (400m). Turn R (200m). ✧

ⓧ *Extension of 1.6 km/1 mile only for Loseley visitors: Turn L on the drive. Only the first part is a public footpath. If going this way, stay on the main drive round R and L bends to Loseley house (800m).*

ⓨ *Depart from the house on the track R of the car park. Just after the car park take the path R into the fields (200m), R over a track, past the pond (400m) and on up the fields to the road (500m). ➧⑤*

④ Keep on through Littleton to the last house L (650m). ✳✳

⑤ Opposite Pillarbox Cottage walk along the drive and continue up the path between fields (400m).

⑥ At the start of the descent take the side path L up under trees past Mount Browne R to houses (600m). Cross the drive and stay ahead down the footpath (250m) then along Sandy Lane past Piccards Manor L to the A3100 opposite **Ye Olde Ship** (350m).

⑦ Turn R up to Ferry Lane L (50m). See St Catherines Chapel on top of he hill then walk down Ferry Lane, across the mouth of the railway tunnel and down to the Navigation towpath (200m). ✳☆

ⓐ *Alternative slightly longer: get to the path opposite (100m) and walk away from the water (200m). Turn R along the edge of Shalford Park (300m), R on the tarmac path over the Tilling Bourne (200m), along the car park (100m) and ahead up the path into the trees (200m). ✣*

ⓑ *Branch R past the back gate of the **Sea Horse** (30m), over the railway (450m), ahead past houses & on the path to the Parrot (350m).*

⑧ Go R along the towpath past St Catherine's Lock (600m), the girder bridge and a pillbox (on the unused embankment) to the road (1000m). Turn L for the *Parrot* (200m).

The railways around Guildford:
The first railway in the region was the LSWR (London & SW Railway) from London to Southampton; it reached Woking in 1838. The branch line from Woking to Guildford opened in 1845, built by the Guildford Junction Railway Co for absorption by the LSWR. The tunnel was built by the LSWR in 1849 to extend this branch to Godalming. In 1859 the Portsmouth Railway Co further extended the Godalming line to Havant where it joined the LBSCR (London, Brighton & South Coast R) line and became the Portsmouth Direct Line for LSWR London trains.

In 1849 the LSWR opened a line from Guildford to Farnham via Tongham. This and the tunnel were used by the RGRR (Reading, Guildford & Reigate Railway) to link the Reading arm N of the Hog's Back with the Reigate arm. This is now called the North Downs Line and has a Gatwick branch. The girder bridge for it arrived by barge.

Soon afterwards, the SER bought the RGRR. The unused embankment (at the pillbox) was intended for a SER spur to the Godalming line. It would have created a shorter route London-Portsmouth but never came into use as it infringed company agreements.

The Horsham & Guildford Direct Railway was opened in 1865 by the LBSCR, to the detriment of the Wey & Arun Junction Canal Co. It closed in 1965 and now provides a route for part of the Downs Link footpath.

The last built was the Waterloo line to Guildford via Effingham Junction, East Horsley and West Clandon, crossing the River Wey at Dapdune. Opened in 1885 it was part of the LSWR's infill with suburban lines after the branch from Woking in 1844. World War I delayed its electrification till 1925.

Railways Centres I P Jowett 1993 240p

20 Shalford Mill and Guildford Castle

8.0 km/5 miles with an extension of 1 km/²⁄₃ mile and a dip into Guildford of 400m; steep slopes; soft sand in summer; bluebells in season; much to see. A good winter walk. OS maps 1:25000 145 Guildford, 1:50000 186 Aldershot.

Start at the bend at the top of Clifford Manor Road, Shalford, TQ 003 480. There is parking behind Shalford Church. On Sundays Millmead car park is free, SU 994 492. Halfpenny Lane car park, TQ 022 484, is close to the walk.

The Sea Horse ☎ 01483 514351
The Weyside ☎ 01483 568024
The Queen Victoria ☎ 01483 566959
The Britannia ☎ 01483 572160

Linking walks 8✳ 12✳ 19✳
21✦ 25✳ 26✿ ⟨9⟩ ✳ ⟨10⟩ ❂

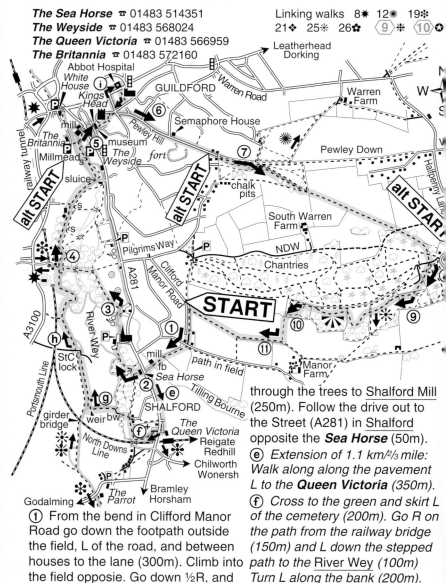

through the trees to Shalford Mill (250m). Follow the drive out to the Street (A281) in Shalford opposite the *Sea Horse* (50m).

ⓔ *Extension of 1.1 km/²⁄₃ mile: Walk along along the pavement L to the* **Queen Victoria** *(350m).*

ⓕ *Cross to the green and skirt L of the cemetery (200m). Go R on the path from the railway bridge (150m) and L down the stepped path to the* River Wey *(100m) Turn L along the bank (200m).*

① From the bend in Clifford Manor Road go down the footpath outside the field, L of the road, and between houses to the lane (300m). Climb into the field opposie. Go down ½R, and

ⓖ *Cross the weir and continue beside the Navigation (400m).*

ⓗ *At St Catherines Lock cross to the tow path and carry on to the next footbridge (650m).* ➔④

② Cross and see the little plaque. Turn R (40m) then L up to the *Sea Horse* top car park and out through the trees to the path (80m). ✳ Go R on the path beside the field and down L (200m), along the car park (100m) and tarmac path over the Tilling Bourne through the trees to Shalford Park (200m).

③ Go L along the edge of the trees (300m) then L on the path to the Godalming Navigation (200m), over the footbridge (70m) and R. ✳

④ Follow the tow path to Millmead Lock in Guildford (1000m).

⑤ Cross the footbridge at the lock and skirt round the theatre to Town Mill (200m). Cross the main road to Rosemary Alley, opposite, and climb the steps to the **King's Head** (50m) (St Mary's Church is L). Turn R up Quarry Street (150m). After the museum go L through the arch in the castle wall, up the narrow road (50m) and L into the castle gardens, up R of the keep and out at the highest point to the 5-way road junction (100m).

ⓘ *If you want to see a bit of Guildford, go L along Tunsgate (100m) and R up High Street (100m). Step into the arch at the Abbot Hospital L then cross the street and go up through Holy Trinity churchyard to the next road (100m). Turn R to the 5-way junction (100m).*

⑥ Walk up Pewley Hill. On top keep on past Semaphore House L, Pewley Hill Reservoir L and (among the houses) Pewley Fort R (800m).

⑦ At the end of the road continue onto Pewley Down, diverging from the L edge to pass the stone column (200m). ✳ ↘ After it (100m) descend obliquely, R of the hedge. Stay ahead between fields to the sandy track (1200m). ❖

⑧ Cross the track and go up into the wood to the next track (NDW) (300m). ◐❖ (If going to Halfpenny Lane car park turn L.) Cross and go straight up to the vehicle track on top (60m). Cross and take the path ½R to the edge of the wood (100m). Cross the field ½L to the path on the brow of the hill (150m). ✳ ↘

⑨ Follow the brow along the Five Fields on Chantries Hill (800m).

⑩ At the little combe descend L, curving R (200m) then go down the R edge of the fields to the major path along the foot (200m).

⑪ Turn R between fields to Clifford Manor Road (700m).

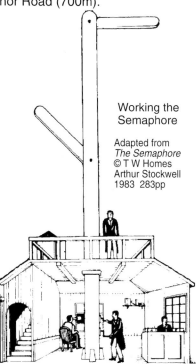

Working the Semaphore

Adapted from
The Semaphore
© T W Homes
Arthur Stockwell
1983 283pp

21 Newlands Corner and St Martha's Hill

About 7.9 km/5 miles with a short cut of 1.1 km/²/₃ mile: A North Downs walk with fine views; three uphill sections; soft sand in summer. OS maps 1:25000 145 Guildford, 1:50000 186 Aldershot.

Start from Newlands Corner car park, TQ 043 492, or one of the St Martha's Hill car parks on Halfpenny Lane, TQ 022 484, or Guildford Lane, TQ 035 485.

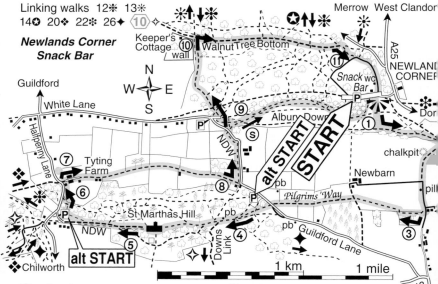

① ⤳ Opposite the snackbar at Newlands Corner car park, walk straight down the grassy hillside to the bottom bridleway (200m). Turn L along it to the broad, oblique, downhill chalky cart track (450m).

② Go down R, round the bend at the pillbox, and on past the chalk pit R, and a farm drive R to the sunken side track L (550m).

③ Just after the side track, ascend the R bank (Lower Greensand). Carry on along the edge of the wood into the field (200m). Turn L but diverge from the edge towards the R corner of the pine plantation below (300m). Cross the path and go up beside the plantation then between fields to the road, Guildford Lane (600m).

④ Continue over the lane in the same direction (100m). ✦ From the car park take one of the uphill converging paths and follow the scarp edge up St Martha's Hill, disregarding numerous side paths. On top pass over the ironstone outcrop and enter the east gate to St Martha's Church (750m). ✧ ⤳

⑤ Leave via the west gate. Go straight down the main track (500m) and diverge R over the grass to the car park (100m). ❖✷

⑥ From the car park cross to the trees R of the road and take the L path on the bank eventually descending to the road (100m). Keep on to the cross track (100m).

⑦ Turn R to Tyting Farm. Go straight past the buildings and on

42

along the sandy track between fields to White Lane (1200m).

⑧ Turn L on the footpath, L of the road behind the trees (400m). At the top end cross the road R and climb the opposite bank (20m).

Ⓢ *Short cut of 1.1 km/¾ mile: Stay ahead up the slope then follow the edge of the wood (1000m) and turn L up to Newlands Corner car park.*

⑨ Turn L (30m) and L again up to White Lane car park (100m). Take the middle of 3 paths into the wood (60m), over a track and eventually down R of a wall (Keepers Cottage) into Walnut Tree Bottom (450m). ✲

⑩ Go R up the valley track until road noise is near (1000m). ✪

⑪ Follow uphill paths R to Newlands Corner car park (350m).

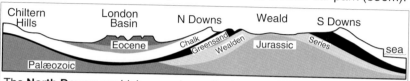

The **North Downs** are high ground on the Chalk along the northern edge of Kent and Surrey into Hampshire, fairly level except where crossed by rivers. At Newlands Corner and the Hogs Back the chalk ridge is narrow. The parallel Greensand ridge appears as lines of hills: St Marthas, Chantries, St Catherines and the Leith Hill range.

These ridges are the broken, eroded edges of the Chalk and Greensand strata, buckled when the Alps were pushed up into a hump by the collision of Europe and Africa tectonic plates. Remnants of the Weald anticline still reach almost to 1000 feet at Leith Hill and Butser Hill in the South Downs. In the middle, where Jurassic rocks almost reach the surface, the thickness of strata removed is more than 1000m (3000+ft), so the Weald would once have been a mountain range.

Greensand is a bad name for the geological stratum which is not always sandy and is rarely green. The name arose from geologists' descriptions when it was first dug. The highest division of the Lower Greensand is the Folkstone Sands which cause the poor soil and heath of St Martha's Hill and yielded the ironstone of the church walls. Below it are the Bargate, the Hythe Sands and the Atherfield Clay.

The steeper south-facing scarp slope of the Downs is caused by erosion of the layer of Gault clay in the Greensand which allows the undermining of the edge of the Chalk. The resulting valley is now dry. The escarpment to the south of the Folkstone Sands is eroded by the tributaries of the River Wey. The contrast here between the adjacent chalk grassland and sandy heath under the same climate is a splendid example of the impact of geology on soil, flora and scenery.

The ice sheet of the Anglian glaciation reached within 80 miles of the Downs so the Weald would have had an ice cap much of the year. Torrents of melt water account for the flints (out of the chalk) in gardens and gravel pits N to the Thames. They piled up as valley deposits which are now the hilltops of the commons and valley bottoms of the Rivers Wey and Blackwater.

The Chalk, Greensand and Wealden beds are the strata of the Cretaceous period which lasted about 80m years and ended 65m years ago. Before and below is the Jurassic; after and above is the Eocene. Strata can be correlated by their fossils throughout the world and the rock types indicate the conditions in which they formed. The spectacular Cretaceous fossils are the dinosaurs but more abundant, widespread, and useful for correlating strata, are the oceanic sea urchins, ammonites and microscopic algæ.

22 Newlands Corner and Silent Pool

About 5.7 km/3½ miles. A short cut of 550m/⅓ mile & extension of 1.6 km/1 mile can be combined; a North Downs walk with fine views; good in winter; one steep ascent and descent. OS maps 1:25000 145 Guildford, 1:50000 186+187.

Start from Newlands Corner car park, TQ 043 492, or from the Silent Pool car park, TQ 059 484, both beside the A25.

Linking walks 12☆ 13☆ 14✿ 16✳ 21✲ 23★ 29☆

Map labels: Merrow West Clandon · NEWLANDS CORNER · Snack Bar wc · P · START · chalkpit · pillbox · NDW · A25 · Newlands Corner Snack Bar · East Cla · alt START · vineyard · pillbox · Silent Pool · Sherbourne Pond · Sherbourne Farm · W Har · N W S · Newbarn · pb · Pilgrims' Way · sand pit landfill · © Crown Copyright MC 100011861 · Guildford Lane · Chilworth Shalford Guildford S · Drummond Arms · mill · ALBURY Farley Green · Tilling Bourne · wall · A248 · A25 · Dor · Sh · Newbarn · 6 · t · s · 5 · 3 · 4 · e · 2 · 1 · f

☇ ✿① At Newlands Corner car park, 50m before the road, take the path ½R over the grass to the A25 (100m) and cross to R of the fence. Follow the North Downs Way, on the level brow of the chalk ridge past a side path slanting back R (1300m) to the crosspath (350m). Turn R downhill (40m).

ⓔ *Extension of 1.6 km/1 mile: Go L on the side path to the downhill path (250m). Descend beside fields to the road (700m). Continue down to the A25 (300m). Cross and go down Upper Street (200m). At the bend (200m) bear R down Chantry Lane to the crosspath (150m).*

ⓕ *Turn R up through the trees to the field (40m). Follow the path down the L edge (200m), up the wood (350m) and down the next field to the A248 (300m). ➔④*

② Stay on the downhill path under trees to the pillbox L (350m) and beside the vineyard (200m) then turn L down the bank to Silent Pool. Go R beside Sherbourne Pond to the far end (80m) and follow the vineyard track and farm drive to the A25, L of the car park (60m).

③ Turn L beside the A25 (100m), then cross and follow the footpath L of the Albury side road, A248, to the track L after the field (200m). ★

④ Turn R aross the A248 into the field. Follow the R edge, over the stream and up into the trees (400m). Continue over the sandpit access road and past the former brickworks R, up to the track (250m) and ahead to the ironstone cottage (150m).

ⓢ *Short cut of 550m/⅓ mile: Turn R along the path between the fields into the trees (300m) and L between the field and road (200m). Stay on the path curving L outside the field at the foot of the downs to the pillbox at the sunken track (350m).*

(t) *Turn R up the track past the junipers R to the car park (500m).*

⑤ Continue ahead on the cart track past houses to the T-junction of sunken Greensand tracks (650m). ✽ Go up the opposite

bank slightly L, and along the edge of the wood into the field R (200m). Turn L but diverge from the edge towards the R corner of the pine plantation below (300m).

⑥ Join the track outside the field and follow it R to Newbarn Farm (150m). Pass L of the house and stay ahead up the path (350m). At Albury Downs, ascend, R of the wood to the car park (250m). ☆

Junipers grow beside the Albury track down from Newlands Corner. *Juniperus communis* is not a neat conical tree like the exotics grown in gardens but an unkempt shrub or small tree with peeling bark and tangled twigs. It looks and feels rather like gorse. It may be the only conifer native in Southern England, as yew is a doubtful native.

The blue/black berries provide the flavour of gin which takes its name from juniper via *jenever*, Dutch, or *genièvre*, French. Gin was devised for medicinal purposes by Dr Sylvius, 1614-72, of Leyden. The oil in the berries is a diuretic. The berries are chiefly collected in the wild in Italy and the Balkans. They are increasingly returning to British cooking but on the continent have long been used as a spice for game and sauerkraut.

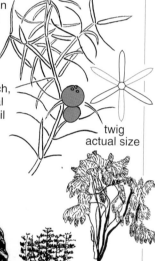

twig
actual size

tree 4m tall

shrub 2m tall

fossil actual size

British Mesozoic Fossils
ed 5 British Museum 1975
© Natural History Museum

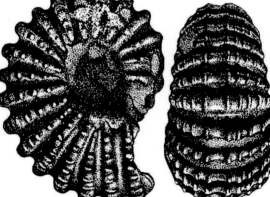

An ammonite, *Douvilleiceras mammillatus*, found in the Gault clay at the former brick-works passed on this walk. The animal existed for less than a million years and rocks elsewhere in the world must be of similar age if they contain this species. It was an oceanic species. useful for world-wide dating. Good quality fossils show the soft parts of an ammonite were like an octopus and the shell was for flotation. Ammonites lived in the Jurassic and Cretaceous geological periods.

23 Silent Pool, North Downs and Shere

About 6 km/3²/₃ miles with a short cut of 550m/¹/₃ mile and an extension of 1.1 km/²/₃ mile; a North Downs walk; one long steep ascent and descent, half shady, good in winter OS maps 1:25000 145 Guildford, 1:50000 187 Dorking.

Start at Silent Pool car park, TQ 059 484, Shere recreation ground, TQ 073 479, or West Hanger car park, TQ 070 493.

Linking 14✿ 16✳ 22★ 24✳ 29◉

The William Bray ☎ 01483 202275
White Horse ☎ 01483 202518

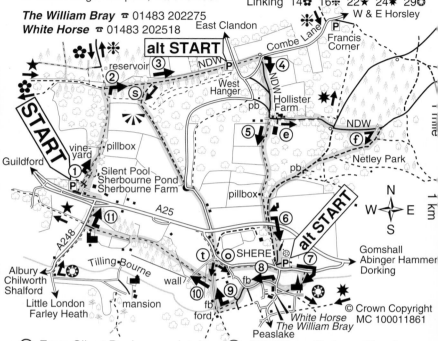

© Crown Copyright MC 100011861

① From Silent Pool car park take the path through the trees and over the <u>vineyard</u> track to <u>Silent Pool</u> (150m). Between the ponds turn L up the bank to the vineyard on the scarp face of the North Downs (100m). Continue up the edge and through the trees to the ridge track (<u>North Downs Way</u>) (500m). ✳✿

② Turn R along the NDW (300m).

Ⓢ *Short cut of 2.1km/¹/₃ mile: At the start of the fields L take the side path R in the trees (200m) and down beside fields (600m). Walk down the road to the A25 (400m). Cross to the path and go on to the road in Shere (200m). At the bend*

Ⓣ *Either bear R down Chantry Lane (150m).* ➔⑩ *or*

Ⓞ *Carry on down the R pavement (of interest for the old cottages) to the middle of the village (500m).* ➔⑦

③ Continue on the NDW to West Hanger car park (600m), over the road and along the path (200m).

④ Turn back R on the road (30m) and take the NDW track L to the L bend at Hollister Farm (400m).

ⓔ *Extension of 1.1 km/²/₃ mile: Turn L with the hard track (NDW) past the farm into the trees on* <u>Netley Heath</u>. *Pass the cross track (450m)* ✳ *and continue to the soft track R at a slight L bend (300m).*

46

(f) *Follow this side track, level at first then increasing steeply downhill (1000m). Before the A25 bridge watch out for a rising path R and go up to the road (50m).* ➔⑥

⑤ Stay ahead on the path down the hill, between the wood L and fields R, to the A25 (700m).

⑥ Cross the road and turn L over the short bridge. Go R down the path above (L of) the sunken track to the car park and the road in Shere (350m). Turn L.

⑦ After the end of Middle Street (200m) take the path R, next the school, over the Tilling Bourne then R of the church. ✪ Keep on out of the churchyard and across the square to the **White Horse** (300m). (The **William Bray** is L.)

⑧ Turn R to the bridge (20m). Don't cross but go L along the lane (Lower Street) beside the Tilling (250m). At the ford, stay ahead on the track L of the bourne (100m). Ignore the vehicle bridge and go on along the narrow field (200m).

⑨ Cross Chantries footbridge and go up the lane past a house (200m).

⑩ At the cross path, turn up through the trees away from the houses. Continue along the edge of the field (wall of Albury Park L) (300m), up through the wood and down the field aiming R of the church, Albury Catholic Apostolic) and out to the road (700m). ★

⑪ Walk along the footpath R to the A25 (200m). Cross and turn L to Silent Pool car park (100m).

Shere in the Domesday Book
actual size
zincograph facsimile
printed by Ordnance
Survey in the *Surrey
Domesday* 1861

The Domesday Book information was compiled for William the Conqueror in 1086. The parchment folios were later sewn together as the book which is on display at the National Archives, Kew. The name was official usage by the 12th century but probably satirical in origin. A register of tax and property for all time would be seen as a tool of tyrannical bureaucracy. An entry starts with the Lord of the Manor. Shere was in the royal demesne so the king was Lord. Edith was the queen of Edward

the Confessor. TRE means before the Conquest, *tempore regis Edwardi*, in the time of King Edward. *A hide* was a variable unit of arable land but 120 acres if defined. Hidage of manors was notional, rating their part of the county tax bill. Entries are grouped by county, then owner, then hundred, uniform in layout and with red highlighting. Clerks could have surfed through it as a database to estimate tax dues but King William's reasons for the survey were not recorded.

Domesday Book and Beyond   F W Maitland CUP 1897 & Fontana 1989

The King holds in demesne ᴱˢSIRA. Edith the queen held it.
Then it responded for ix hides: however there were then xvi hides there. Now it does not pay tax. Land for xiiii ploughs. In the demesne are ii ploughs. xix villeins & vi bordars with xii ploughs. There is a church; vi slaves. ii mills @ x shillings; iii acres of pasture. Woodland @ L pigs.
TRE & later & now value xv pounds.

24 Shere, Netley Heath and Abinger Hammer

About 9.0 km/5½ miles with a short cut of 750m km/½ mile over Hackhurst Down, omitting Abinger Hammer; good all the year round; one long ascent; shady in summer. OS maps 1:25000 145 Guildford; 1:50000 187 Dorking.

Start at Shere car park, TQ 073 479, or at Francis Corner car park, TQ 077 496.

The William Bray ☎ 01483 202275   Linking walks 16✴ 17✿ 23✹ 29◇ 34❖
The White Horse ☎ 01483 202518   35✴ 40★ 7✛ 20✳
The Compasses ☎ 01483 202506
Gomshall Mill ☎ 01483 203060

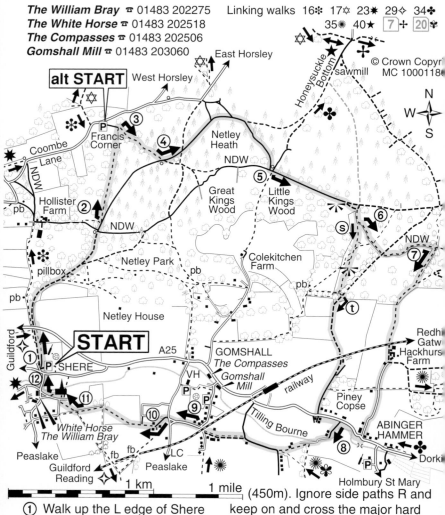

© Crown Copyr
MC 1000118

(450m). Ignore side paths R and

① Walk up the L edge of Shere recreation ground above the sunken byway (300m). ✳ At the A25, cross the road then the sunken byway. Continue up L of the byway (30m) then join the byway and ascend into Netley Heath past a pillbox R

keep on and cross the major hard track, North Downs Way (350m).

② After the cross track (60m) join the diverging side track L. Stay on it until it bends L (to Francis Corner car park) (650m). ✿

③ Turn R on the hard path (400m).

④ Bear L down the hard track to a side track from the road (400m). ✿ Carry on, curving R past another (150m), and past a diverging bridle-way (100m) ❖✛ to the end (400m).

⑤ Turn L on the hard track, NDW, through Little Kings Wood (550m). Bear R on the diverging side track (50m) then turn R on the side path (NDW/Hackhurst Downs)(100m).

Ⓢ *Shorter by 750m/½ mile: At the twist, stay ahead over the brow (200m) and steeply down (300m).*

Ⓣ *Outside, descend L (30m) then go down the track (400m). Pass under the railway and over a rise to the A25 (400m). Cross to the pavement and turn L (150m). ➤⑧*

⑥ At the twist bear L (250m). Cross the straight sloping track and stay on the winding path to the downhill path (400m). ♣

⑦ Descend R (300m). Join the converging path and keep on down over the railway (400m). ✳ After Hackhurst Farm follow the lane over the hill and down to the A25 in Abinger Hammer (700m). Cross to the pavement and go R (200m).

⑧ Opposite the old house (with Horsham slab roof) take the lane winding L of houses and over the Tilling Bourne (300m). Continue up the path beside the garden (200m) and along the drive from the houses L. When the drive bends R (250m) stay ahead on the path and track through the farm to the next road (300m).

⑨ Turn R under the railway (40m) and L up the road (200m). Fork down R at the split end.

⑩ Cross to Gravelpits Lane and follow it round L (130m). Before the last house, turn R up to the fields. Stay ahead to the cross path above Shere Church (600m). ✧

⑪ Bear R down between the fields (200m). Cross the churchyard and square L to the **White Horse** ✳ (150m). The **William Bray** is 50m L

⑫ Cross the Tilling Bourne and go on to the T-junction (200m). Turn L & R or R & L for the car park.

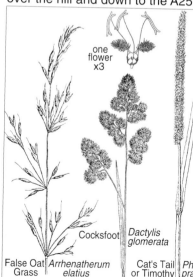

one flower x3

Cocksfoot *Dactylis glomerata*

False Oat *Arrhenatherum* Grass *elatius*

Cat's Tail *Phleum* or Timothy *pratense*

Grass is widely perceived as one kind of plant but there are 150 grasses in Britain and 10,000 species worldwide. The three shown are 100cm tall and the most easily recognized large British grasses. Their inflorescences are made up of numerous small flowers which are not colourful because they are wind pollinated.

The flowers are visible at the time of pollination. Stamens hang out of the heads in 3s. Stigmas protrude like tiny cotton wool buds to sieve the air.

The family is highly significant. They cover much of the land, provide food for many animals and include cereals, on which most of mankind depend. There are at least 150 *Bambusa spp.*, many used in buildings. In the wrong places, grasses are weeds.

25 Shalford and Chinthurst Hill

About 8.2 km/5 miles, Lower Greensand and Wey navigation; mainly farmland; one short steep hill. OS maps 1:25000 145 Guildford, 1:50000 186 Aldershot.

Start at Shalford, parking in the side road next to *The Parrot*, SU 998 467, or at Chinthurst Hill car park, TQ 014 462, or at Trunley Heath Road, SU 999 462. Shalford railway station is close to the walk route.

Linking walks 8✦ 9✿ 20✳ 26✳
⟨9⟩✳ ⟨10⟩★ ⟨11⟩✦ ⟨36⟩☆

The Queen Victoria ☎ 01483 566959
The Sea Horse ☎ 01483 514351
The Parrot ☎ 01483 561400

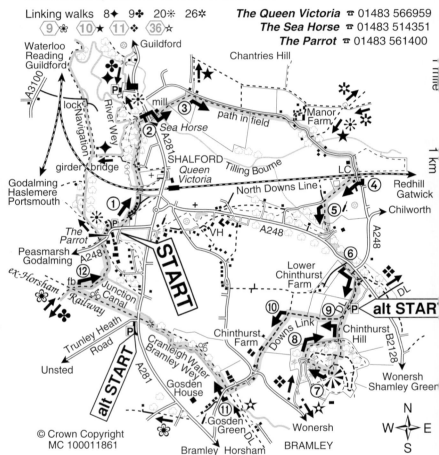

© Crown Copyright MC 100011861

① From the **Parrot**, in Shalford cross the main road, the A248. Opposite the side road take the oblique path over the green to the houses (200m). Follow the track round the houses (200m). Cross the railway. ✦ Keep on to the cross path (150m) then use the lesser path L of the main path (350m).✳

② Just before the track junction turn R through the **Sea Horse** gate. Cross the car park and turn R on the pavement (40m). At the WWII barrier slot (& tiny plaque) R, cross the A281 and follow the drive to Shalford Mill (see the firemarks over the arch) (70m). Go over the Tilling and up the field (250m). ★✳

50

③ Don't join the lane here but turn along the hedge R of the lane from field to field (650m). Join the lane, just before the house, and carry on, down over the Tilling Bourne (300m) and up over the North Downs Line level crossing (400m).

④ Turn R beside the railway (30m) and bear L on the oblique path across the sports fields of Guildford Royal Grammar School (200m).

⑤ At the end don't join the lane but turn L over the grass. Aim for the gap at the R end of the hedge (150m). Keep on ahead, over the brook to the road (100m). Turn L along the pavement (200m). ❖

⑥ Cross into the drive of Lower Chinthurst Farm (40m). Turn L on the track outside the boundary to the next path, next to a house (150m). Go R on the path up past the car park L (250m). Ascend between fields to the Chinthurst Hill boundary (200m). Bear L beside the steps then keep to uphill paths to the tower on top (250m). ↘

With your back to the tower doorway, Winterfold Hill is almost ahead (SE) in the distance with Pitch, Holmbury and Leith Hills behind it. The houses below, slightly L are Wonersh. Above them is Barnett Hill with eponymous house protruding from the trees. Far R, the South Downs may be visible.

⑦ From the door, go to the back of the tower and down the main steep path to the tarmac drive (200m). ✦

⑧ At the hairpin bend follow the little path R to the edge of the hill (100m) and on beside fields ↘ to

To the north, Guildford Cathedral is visible through the notch in the North Downs cut by the River Wey. Right of the notch, the Downs are hidden by Chantries and St Martha's Hills. Where they reappear, cars can be seen ascending to Newlands Corner.

the path from the car park (300m).

⑨ Go down the path (150m). Before the car park, turn L on the Downs Link side path (400m).

⑩ Go round the L bend and down to the road junction (500m). Ahead down the road opposite (30m), ❀ join the drive up L. Carry on beside the road, soon below it. Keep R to the cycle track (Downs Link and fomer Horsham Railway) (200m).

⑪ Turn R under the arch. Watch out for and follow the small path L on the river bank (700m). Rejoin the track, crossing the A281(100m) and the River Wey (500m). ❖✳

⑫ Drop to the river bank. Follow it away from the wood past the Junction Canal (250m) to the A248 at Shalford (250m). Cross to the pavement. Go over the bridge and round to the *Parrot* (100m).

Firemarks were fixed on buildings to indicate they were insured. They are now collectables and some have been put up on walls as ornaments by later owners. Many of the surviving ones are cast lead with stamped numbers but brass, iron, zinc and stucco ones were also issued, usually about 30cm tall and brightly painted when new. The earliest were made for *The Fire Office* in London which became *Phoenix*) around 1680. Fire insurance companies initiated many of the town fire brigades later taken over by local government, in some cases, not until the 20th century.

British Fire Marks 1680-1875 Brian Wright 1982 Woodhead-Faulkner 480pp

26 Chilworth Gunpowder Works

About 7.4 km/4½ miles with a steep uphill short cut of 2.1 km/1¼ miles; a scenic walk with much to see; two bluebell woods; soft sand in summer; good in winter. OS maps 1:25000 145 Guildford, 1:50000 186 Aldershot.

Start from one of the St Martha's Hill car parks, Guildford Lane, TQ 035 485, or Halfpenny Lane, TQ 022 484, or from the kerbside near the *Percy Arms* in Chilworth, TQ 030 473. Chilworth railway station is close to the route.

Linking walks 12✦ 20✿ 21✦ 25✳ 27✳ ⟨10⟩✿ ⟨12⟩✤

The Percy Arms ☎ 01483 561765

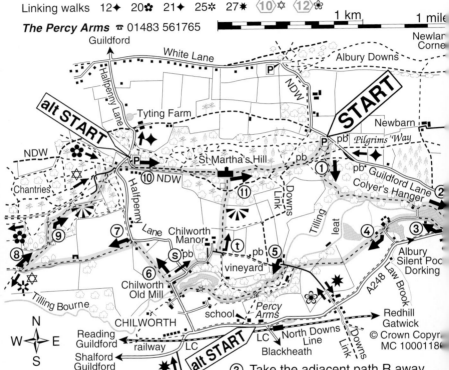

① Walk away from Guildford Lane on the path branching L from the car park over the cross path on the edge of the escarpment (50m). Go down the steep narrow, winding path through beech wood, Colyer's Hanger, with hillside L and river below R, to the cottage (1000m).
② At the bottom turn L on the path away from the drive, round L of Waterloo Pond. Continue through a garden and along the drive past more houses to the A248 (300m).✤

③ Take the adjacent path R away from the road, between the Tilling Bourne and Waterloo Pond (250m). On the drive (ancient dam), go L to the last building at Postford Pond (Postford Mill until 1996) (250m).
④ After the bridge, take the footpath L of the cottage drive. Continue over fields (gunpowder mills) to the vehicle track (700m).✳
⑤ Turn R. Ignore the path L at the mill leat bridge R but take the side path L just before the Tilling (80m). Almost immediately branch R to the

52

bourn (20m) and follow it past the incorporating mill ruins L. Go round a L bend to the main path (200m). Turn R past the footbridge L over the leat (60m) (path to the **Percy Arms** *400m)*. Stay on the main path, over several branch leats, to Blacksmith Lane (550m). Turn R over spillways to the bend near Chilworth Old Mill (100m).✿♣

ⓢ *Short cut of 2.1 km/1¼ mile with a very steep ascent. Turn R on Halfpenny Lane to the bend (120m) and go straight up the Chilworth Manor drive past the manor house gateway L and the field R (250m).*

ⓣ *Turn R on the track above the field (50m) then L up the footpath beside fields.* ↘↗ *Continue steeply up St Martha's Hill to the church on top (500m).✦ Turn R.* ➤⑪

⑥ Go L up the footpath beside Old Mill to Halfpenny Lane (400m).

⑦ Turn into the field L. Follow the L edge into a dip (400m), over the rise (200m) and down (200m). ✳

⑧ Take the path back R up the field and bear L up through trees to the cross path on the brow (450m).

⑨ Go R (200m), into the next field (100m), ½L over the top field (100m), through the trees R before the track and up R of the house (200m).

⑩ Walk L up the road (30m) and R up the side path. Stay ahead to the top of St Martha's Hill (700m) and through the churchyard (80m). ↘↗

⑪ Go out at the east gate and straight down the broad sandy path on the edge of the hill past many side paths (450m). After the pillbox, curve L to the car park (300m).

Mills in the Guildford area in the 19th century were mostly papermills. Many replaced waterwheels with turbines as technology advanced. In 1822 William Cobbett contrasted Chilworth's beauty with the industry of its mills: *two of the most damnable purposes namely the making of gunpowder and banknotes.*

Traditional paper is made of cellulose, the most abundant organic substance in nature. Plants form cellulose in their cell walls. Its tensile strength permits such remarkable structures as grass stems 2m tall and trees 100m tall.

Egyptian documents have lasted 4½ thousand years. Papyrus is plant cells, strips of compressed pith from a Nile sedge, *Cyperus papyru.* Paper made from linen rags was commonplace by the time of Chaucer (d. 1400). From the 1740s the Lancashire cotton mills augmented the supply of rags. Paper-mills drove machinery for stirring and rolling and consumed lots of water. Wood pulp superseded rags around 1880. Chemical processing eliminated lignin from the wood cells and steam power was needed to satisfy demand.

Cellulose in cell walls is in the form of microfibrils 3nm wide that are bundles of about 36 cellulose molecules. (1 nanometer = $^1/_{1,000,000}$ mm).

Cellulose molecules are made up of repeated units ie it is a polymer. The units are β-glucose in chains up to 1,000 long. Starch is also a polymer but of α-glucose. These are isomers; that is to say, molecules with the same atoms but arranged differently

Isomers

α-glucose β-glucose   fructose

Most of the energy residing in a plant is in its cellulose but animals cannot digest it. Ruminants and termites use symbiotic microbes to break it down.

Fabric conditioners contain cellulase enzymes obtained from fungi. New cotton is glossy but fibres get scraped exposing a fuzz of molecule ends which are trimmed by the enzymes.

Cellophane film and rayon yarn are biodegradable plastics manufactured from reconstituted natural cellulose.

27 Blackheath, Great Tangley and Chilworth

About 6.9 km/4⅓ miles. The extension of 550m/⅓ mile and short cut of 1 km/⅔ mile may be used together. Long views, undulating. The Blackheath tracks are confusing. OS maps 1:25000 145 Guildford, 1:50000 186 Aldershot.

Start from Blackheath village ▬ car park, TQ 036 462, or in Chilworth, at the kerbside near the *Percy Arms*, TQ 030 473. Chilworth Station is near the walk.

Percy Arms ☎ 01483 561765

Linking walks   26✳   28✿   32☆
⟨10⟩✳ ⟨11⟩✿ ⟨12⟩✛

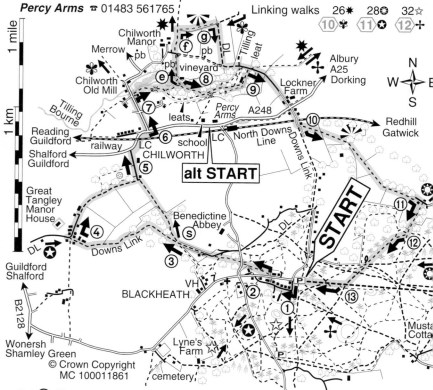

✿☆① From the exit of Blackheath car park, follow the track round behind the houses (200m).

② After the track from the cricket pavilion (30m), take the path R between gardens to the road (50m). Cross and turn L on the diverging path (80m). Fork L, skirt round the corner of a garden and cross the road (150m). Stay ahead to the vehicle track (200m). Follow it (L) (100m), to the very oblique cross path (150m).

Ⓢ *Short cut of 1 km/⅔ mile: Bear R on the bridleway, down to the cottage at the bottom (550m).* ➤⑤

③ Go straight on (Downs Link) eventually winding down to the track junction between houses at Great Tangley (900m).

④ Turn R on the track past buildings. Keep going below fields to the next house (650m). Turn L.

⑤ Follow the drive out to the A248 in Chilworth (200m) and turn R over the level crossing (250m).

⑥ Turn L down Blacksmith Lane to the Gunpowder Mill path R, next to the end house R (250m).

⑦ Follow the main path (250m). On the 2nd R curve) take the 1st L side path to the bridge (100m).

ⓔ *Hilly extension of ½ km/⅓ mile: Cross and follow the bank of the Tilling Bourne (50m). Cross that. Go up the bank and straight up outside the vineyard (Chilworth Manor house visible far L) (200m). Cross the track and go on up the St Martha's Hill path (170m).* ✱

ⓕ *Turn R up into the second field and follow the bottom edge (300m).*

ⓖ *At the end join the track below. Follow it down between the fields (300m), round a L bend and down over two bridges (200m).* ➔⑨

⑧ Don't cross but turn R to rejoin the main path (150m). Keep on (L) past the footbridge R (40m) *(Vera's path to the **Percy Arms**: 250m to the A248 & 150m L).*

Continue along the main path, L of the mill leat, disregarding L turns. Pass R of the incorporating mill ruins to the end of the path at the track (350m). Cross the bridge R. ✛

⑨ Keep on up past Lockner Farm and over the A248 (400m). Go up the drive between the houses and over the railway bridge (150m).

⑩ Turn L into the field and diverge from the railway. Climb the lynchet to the next field and aim for the top corner (400m) (see St Marthas Hill behind). In the next field follow the path into the valley and up beside a line of trees to the cottage (700m). ✪

⑪ After the garden, climb the bank R. Go up the path between fields into Blackheath Common (250m).

⑫ At the complex junction take the ½R path up the valley side (80m) then bear L. Keep on up (300m), over several cross tracks until you see the car park R (200m). Turn R to it (200m).

Great Tangley Manor House is a fine, moated Tudor house but only gables can be seen from the public paths. The façade has 1582 incised in the timbers but it was a new front on an old house; decorative curved braces are characteristic of eastern England. The estate was probably carved from the great Domesday Book manor of Bramley; a Walter de Tangley is listed in court records in the 13th century. *Great* was added to the name in the 17th century, when the estate was divided. The drawing by Margaret Palmer is from *Wonersh - A guide to its principal buildings* © Wonersh Hist Soc 1996

28 Albury Heath and Village

About 7.7 km/4¾ miles on the Lower Greensand with an alternative section and short cut of 1.6 km/1 mile; hilly farmland, heath and woods, shady; soft sand in summer. OS 1:25000 145 Guildford, 1:50000 186 Aldershot +187 Dorking.

Start from the cricket field car park on Albury Heath, TQ 050 470, or find a kerbside parking spot in the village.

Linking walks
27❀ 29❖ 30❀ 31❀ ⟨12⟩❖

The Drummond Arms ☎ 01483 202039
The William IV ☎ 01483 202685

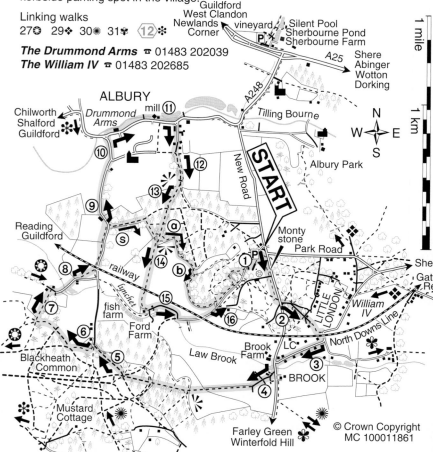

© Crown Copyright
MC 100011861

❖❀① From the parking area walk along the edge of the cricket field near the road watching out for the Monty stone L just before the track (150m). Continue along the edge of the heath (200m) then cross the road to the broad track opposite.

② Walk away from the road (80m) and turn R down the side track to the house (150m). Pass L of the house, down the footpath to the road (100m). ❀

③ Walk under the railway bridge and down the road to the junction in Brook hamlet (400m). ❀

④ Turn L across Law Brook (60m) and R on the first track, up past the side tracks and paddocks (200m).

At the L bend, take the side track R beside the hedge. Continue up into the pines (400m) then straight and level (250m), over a cross track, to the junction of 6 radiating tracks in Blackheath Common (200m).

⑤ Fork R on the track over the brow of the hill and down to the house (300m).

⑥ Turn back up the sunken path round the top of the garden to the 4-way junction (200m). ✿✱ Bear R (150m). Cross a cart track and go on down into the valley (150m).

⑦ Turn R down the valley path, out of the wood and between fields to the cottage (250m). Go R, down the lane, over Law Brook and up to the R curve (200m).

⑧ Just round the bend at the top, bear L up the field to the top R corner (150m). Cross the railway lines and carry on, above the rocky chasm containing the road, to the end of the path (300m).

Ⓢ *Short cut of 1.6 km/1 mile: Over the lane go up the forest track (300m).Take the side track R to the end of the wood (200m).* ➔⑭ *or* ➔ⓐ

⑨ Walk down the road L to the end in the village of Albury (600m).

⑩ Follow the pavement R through the village past the **Drummond Arms** L (100m) and Albury Mill L (300m) to the L curve (150m).

⑪ Turn R into the estate yard. If the office is open ask to see the pigeon house then walk to the top of the drive and on up the track to the junction in the trees (200m).

⑫ Climb to the corner of the field above L and follow the edge above the sunken track (200m), Rejoin the track near the top and turn L.

⑬ Almost immediately, bear R out of the sunken path over the cross track on top (200m) and down to the corner of the wood (250m). Enter the field and turn L.

ⓐ *Alternative of equal length on forest paths: Turn onto the path L inside the edge of the wood. Follow it round and down outside the big field to the cleft (400m).*

ⓑ *Pass R of the valley field and up round a knoll to the steep side path from the lane R (450m).* ➔⑯

⑭ Go straight down the field (350m). Cross the railway to the sunken path in the trees (50m) and go round L past Ford Farm (100m).

⑮ Follow the drive between the buildings (250m). Turn L on the lane to the railway bridge (150m) and up to steep side paths L & R (150m). Go up the L bank (30m).

⑯ Follow the edge above the lane to the sandpit (150m). Go L outside the pit round to the cricket pavilion (200m) and the car park (100m).

Leaf length distinguishes pines from other conifers; the needles are always longer than 5cm/2" and usually longer than 10cm/4". There are no species native to southern England though more than thirty have been introduced, mostly as ornamentals. Some of these have needles in 3s or 5s. In Britain only two pines are used for forestry on sand: Scots pine, *Pinus sylvestris*, with short twisted needles and 5cm cones and Corsican pine, *Pinus nigra* var *maritima*, with needles about 12 cm and cones about 7cm long.

Scots pine

Corsican pine

actual size

29 Shere, Little London and Albury Park

About 8.4 km/5¼ miles with short cuts of 400m and 2.9 km/1¾ miles.
A scenic Greensand walk; undulating with several short ascents; good in winter.
OS maps 1:25000 145 Guildford, 1:50000 187 Dorking.

Start from Albury Heath car park (cricket field), TQ 050 470, or Shere recreation
ground car park, TQ 073 479, or the roadside at Shere church, or HC7 heath car
park, TQ 071 469. Silent Pool car park, TQ 059 484 is close to the walk.

Linking 22✫ 23✪ 24◆ 28❖ 30❀ 31✦　　***The White Horse*** ☎ 01483 202518
　　　　　　　　　　　　　　　　　　　　The William Bray ☎ 01483 202275
　　　　　　　　　　　　　　　　　　　　The William IV ☎ 01483 202685

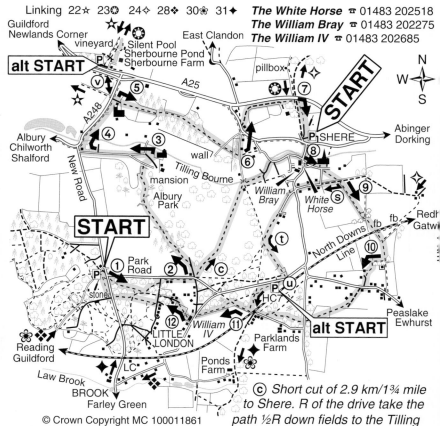

© Crown Copyright MC 100011861

① Outside Albury Heath car park, just R of Park Road, take the oblique path through the trees and keep on across the heath (250m). Bear L on the curving track (30m) and L again on the side path (130m). Join the road L (20m) and turn R on the path beside it to the bend (200m). Cross the road to the drive of Albury Park (250m).

ⓒ *Short cut of 2.9 km/1¾ mile to Shere. R of the drive take the path ½R down fields to the Tilling (700m). Continue R of the bourne, on path, then track then road to the bridge in Shere (600m).* ↦⑧ *ahead*

② Go along the drive past the lodge (100m) then curve L & R on the footpath. Stay ahead to the top of the slope (300m) and down to the tarmac drive (800m). Cross the grass to Albury Old Church next to the Tilling Bourne (100m).

③ Depart from the church gate ahead over the grass (100m) and along the drive to the A248 (400m).

④ Walk along the pavement R over the bourne and up past Albury Catholic Apostolic Church (300m) to the cross path (100m). ★✿

ⓥ *To visit Silent Pool, stay ahead and cross the dual carriageway to the car park (250m) then return.*

⑤ Go up the cart track to the fields (100m), straight up to the top L corner (200m) ↘ and into the trees on the little Greensand ridge. Continue down to the field (400m), along the R edge (150m), over the drive into the trees and down to the sunken lane (150m).

⑥ Walk up the lane L to the road (150m). Cross and turn L up the pavement (50m). After the lodge turn R on the Manor drive. Follow it round a field near the A25 (350m). At the bend to the house R, stay ahead on the path under trees to the cleft with the sunken track under the A25 (100m). ✧

⑦ Cross the sunken track on the A25 (50m) then turn R on the path in the trees above the track to the recreation field (150m) and keep on down to the bottom (100m). From Shere recreation ground car park go out from either end to the road junction (100m). Walk through the village on Middle Street and over the Tilling Bourne bridge to the **White Horse** (150m). (The **William Bray** is 50m further on.) Turn L.

⑧ Cross the triangular square into the churchyard (120m). R of the church, turn R to the road (25m) and L to the side road (20m). Take the path L of Church Hill, obliquely up to the cross track (150m).

ⓢ *Short cut of 400 m/¼ mile: Turn R on the track (100m). Continue ahead down the lane, Spinning Walk (200m), over the road, up Pathfields, over the hill (200m), down the path between fields and up to a junction (200m).*

ⓣ *Take the path up L (20m) and fork L up to the road (300m).*

ⓤ *Cross to the heath. Follow the path L of HC7 car park (100m), down to the cross path (150m). Turn L to the railway (100m). ✦❀ Don't cross it but turn R. ✦⑪*

⑨ Go straight up the path (400m), over the railway and on to the trees at the top of the R field (200m).

⑩ Turn R on the side path beside the field (100m) then L up past houses to the road (150m). Slightly R (25m) take the track on the other side between gardens (100m). The path curves R behind the gardens and continues between fields to the next road (400m). Stay ahead through the trees opposite (250m) then turn L to the lane near houses (50m). Go R to the bend (100m) ✦ and cross the railway lines.

⑪ Stay ahead (150m). Just after the corner of the field, turn L on the cross path beside the field to the road at Little London (250m). ❖

⑫ Cross to the **William IV** and go round to the car park (80m). From the R corner cross the little fields obliquely to the vehicle track in the trees (100m). Go L to the heath (150m), L along the edge (100m) then R straight across (150m), over the track, through the trees and over the road (150m) to the Monty stone, 20m R. Keep on along the edge of the cricket field to the parking area (100m).

30 **Farley Heath and Brook**

About 7.3 km/4½ miles with an extension of 2 km/1¼ mile to Little London and
the William IV; rolling hills on the Greensand: woodland and heath; lots of stiles;
soft sand in summer. OS maps 1:25000 145 Guildford, 1:50000 187 Dorking.

Start from Farley Heath car park (HC8), TQ 051 448,
or, on the extension, from Albury
cricket field car park, TQ 060 466.

28✳ 29❀ 31✳ 32✧
33✿ 34✳ ⑫✩

The William IV
☎ 01483 202685

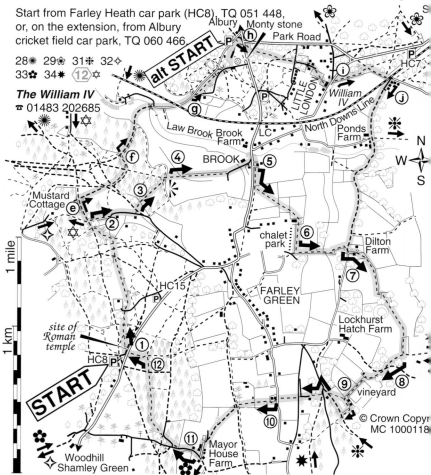

✧① Start down the track from the
low gateway of HC8. Immediately
diverge L on the path over the
Roman temple, through bracken to
the wider path (120m). Stay ahead
over a drive (180m), R of the house
(80m) and over two horse tracks to
a T-junction (400m). Bear L to the
horse track in the dip (150m) and
turn R, past a little field (50m). ✩✳

ⓔ *Extension of 2 km/1 mile via
Little London and the William IV:
Carry on ahead up the slope to the
forest track from the gate L (180m).
Turn R. Cross three level tracks
(400m) and descend to the valley
path, still in forest (120m).*
ⓕ *Go down the valley (400m),
along the lane (150m), up under the
railway to steep side paths (150m).*

60

ⓖ Turn up the R bank. Keep to uphill paths above the lane to the track on the flat top (250m). Go L to the cricket field (100m) and make for the far end (N) (200m).

ⓗ *From the cricket field, cross the road to the oblique heath path R of Park Road. Follow it to the wider track (250m) and carry on to the unmade road (100m).* ❧ *Cross that and go on along the track between houses (150m) then ½R over little fields to the* **William IV** *(150m).*

ⓘ *Just up the road (20m) take the path ½R outside the field (250m). At the cross track turn R, still near the field. Cross the railway (150m).*

ⓙ *Turn R past houses. Continue on the track past Ponds Farm R (450m), over Law Brook (80m) and up to Dilton Farm L (750m).* ➔⑦

② Turn R on the cross path towards the house (150m) and continue along the drive (150m).

③ Opposite the next house go up the L bank, over the converging track (20m) and along the path through trees to the fields (300m).

④ Go straight down the fields to the track (450m) and down L to the road at Brook (150m). ✳

⑤ Turn R up the road (60m) and L into the drive after the houses. Follow the footpath up above the road to the fields on the brow of the hill (200m). Turn L obliquely across the paddocks, aiming for the far end of the distant large barn (400m). Go round L of the barn (50m) and up beside a field (200m).

⑥ Stay on the path round the end of the field, down through the small wood and around the zigzag edge of the next field to the track (350m). Go up the track R (30m).

⑦ Turn L on the tarmac drive to Dilton Farm (50m). Enter the field R after Black House. Cross the L corner and follow the hedge up the hill (350m). When the fence bends L into a corner, cross into the trees but continue in the same direction, up over the foot of the hillock and towards the large house (450m). ✳

⑧ On the path outside the top field turn R down into the trees (150m). Join a converging bridleway (50m) then fork L up to fields near a barn (100m). Enter the field L and go along the R edge past the vineyard into the next, steep field (200m).

⑨ If allowed, cross to the bottom R corner (120m). If not, go L along the top past the house (80m), down R outside the field (70m) and R down the track (200m). At the track junction turn back L on the forest track. Immediately, bear R on the level path (40m) then turn R over the brook and up through the trees. After the house continue on the drive to the bend (150m) then cross the sunken track and keep on between fields to the road (150m).

⑩ L of the barn (20m) take the path skirting the garden, between paddocks (150m) and ahead over the sunken track (300m). Up in the field follow the track up to the farmyard (350m) and go out L to the (unmade) road (120m). ✿

⑪ Go R past the houses and up the slope (150m). Bear R on the first track into the wood (150m). When it bends R, stay ahead on the small path down through the wood to a track (450m) and over it to the next cross path (120m).

⑫ Turn L up to the road, opposite Farley Heath car park (150m).

31 Albury Heath and Peaslake

About 8.7 km/5½ miles with a woodland extension of 1.5 km/1 mile: farmland and woods on the Lower Greensand, hilly, long views, lots of stiles.
OS maps 1:25000 145 Guildford, 1:50000 187 Dorking.

Park on Albury Heath beside the wide side track on the brow above the railway, TQ 061 466, or in Peaslake car park behind the inn car park, TQ 086 448.

Hurtwood Inn ☎ 01306 730769
The William IV ☎ 01483 202685

Linking Walks 28❀ 29✦ 30❋
34★ 35✿ 36★ 40✿

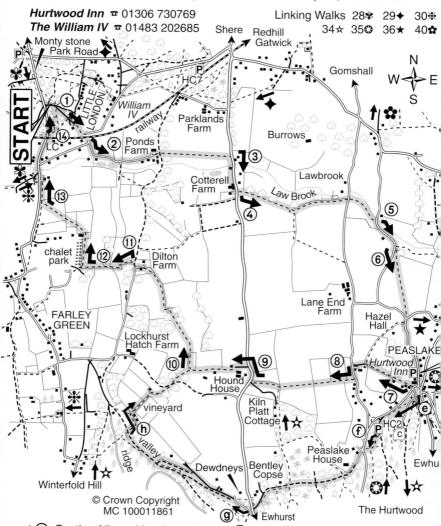

© Crown Copyright
MC 100011861

✦① On the Albury Heath track walk away from the road (80m). Bear R on the side track (150m). Stay ahead on track and path L of the house down to the road (150m).

② Go under the railway (50m) and along the drive (L) to Ponds Farm (600m). At the end, continue on the path across the sunken track (50m) and straight over the field (500m).

62

③ Walk down the road R, across Lawbrook valley and up (250m).

④ Just before the fine house R, Cotterell, take the path L between fields to the next road (800m). In the field opposite, carry on along the Law Brook valley side and up by the hedge to the road (250m).

⑤ Turn R along the road swinging L then R, to two adjacent side paths L on the R curve (300m). ❀

⑥ Take the 2nd path up the middle of the field to the road junction (450m) ★ and the road ahead, past Hazel Hall, down to Peaslake and the **Hurtwood Inn** (500m). ☆❂

ⓔ *Extension of 1½ km/1 mile: Opposite the inn, go up the drive past the church and round R (150m). At the L curve diverge R on the side path R into the valley (150m) and bear L through the car park (Hurtwood Control 2)(150m).*

ⓕ *At the top, take the side path R up to the road (120m). Turn L and fork R up Peaslake House drive (150m). At the R bend stay ahead up the track into the wood (500m). After the cross path in the dip, join the path L of the track and keep on to the next road (300m).*

ⓖ *Cross and go up Dewdneys drive (150m). If dry, bear L on the bridleway (600m). If wet stay on the drive (350m) and, before fields, bear L down the side track (300m). Continue down the valley (300m).*

ⓗ *Turn R outside the next field up towards the house (60m) then L along the top. Halfway along (80m), turn into the gateway. Follow the L hedge past the vineyard to the end (250m). Outside, drop into the dip R (150m). Fork L up to fields and the side path L on top (150m).* ➔⑩

⑦ Cross the front of the inn (50m) and go up the footpath beside the 1st house. Stay ahead along the L edge of the fields on top ⬈ and down the Quakers' Orchard drive to the road (400m). Turn L (100m).

⑧ Take the track R before the house. Stay ahead between fields, into a little valley and up round the R edge to the next road (750m).

⑨ Walk down the road R (150m) and into the drive beside the gate of Hound House (100m). At the end skirt the garden and go on between fields, past a big house above L (200m) to the side path R (100m).✴

⑩ Go down the edge of the small field (100m), down the large field, through the trees to the next field (350m) and down the R edge towards Dilton Farm (350m). Cut the corner to the black house. Join the drive and go out L (60m).

⑪ Walk down the track R (40m) and take the path L which zigzags back around the end of the field (200m). Go up through the trees and on beside the field (200m).

⑫ At the next corner disregard the path ahead and turn R, between the field and chalet park, down to the barn (200m). Go round the R end of the barn to the field (50m) and ½L across the paddocks to the distant hedge corner (400m).

⑬ Follow the path above the sunken road down to the house (150m). ❀ Go down the road, over Law Brook and up to the North Downs Line level crossing (300m).

⑭ Just over the railway, take the steep path R up on the heath (60m) and one of the side paths L up to the track. Turn L to the starting place (150m).

32 Shamley Green and Blackheath

About 8.1 km/5 miles with short cuts of 1.9 km/1¼ miles and 900 m/½ mile.
Farmland and heath on the Greensand; short steep slopes; shade; long views,
soft sand in summer. OS maps 1:25000 145 Guildford, 1:50000 186 Aldershot.

Start from Shamley Green crossroads, TQ 032 438 (park beside Woodhill Lane)
or from Blackheath village car park, TQ 036 462.

Linking walks   27☆   30◇   33❖
⟨11⟩✳   ⟨12⟩✳   ⟨36⟩✳   ⟨37⟩✳   ⟨39⟩✦

The Bricklayers Arms ☎ 01483 898377
The Red Lion ☎ 01483 892202

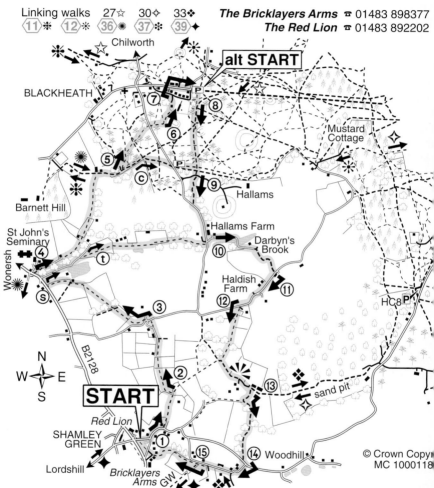

① From the crossroad at <u>Shamley Green</u> walk along Woodhill Lane (250m). At the end of the first R curve take the path L up beside the house drive (250m).

② In the top field turn L along the edge (50m) then cross parallel with the L edge (150m). Carry on in the next field (70m) then R of the farm drive (120m). Join the drive. Go over the brow and down to the L bend (300m). Either continue to the bottom or go down the path R to the road (50m) then L (20m).

③ Opposite the drive take the path above the road until level with the little ridge R (100m) then bear R over the field below the ridge to 50m L of the corner trees (200m). Go on down the next field to the bottom corner (250m) and along the edges to the dangerous road exit (300m). Walk down the road R. ✳

⑤ *Short cut of 1.9 km/1¼ miles boggy in winter: At the first drive R (60m) turn R. Keep on round the bend near the house (250m).*

ⓣ *After the bend (100m) enter the R field. Diverge from the R edge, aiming just R of the house above (300m). Stay ahead up the sunken path between fields and through the wood to the road (600m). Turn L (20m) then R.* ♦⑩

④ Just before the 2nd drive R (120m) take the path R. After waste ground, follow the tarmac drive (R) (St John's Seminary L) to the house (250m). Keep on along the path to the next house (200m), through the garden and small fields and up to the T-junction at houses (450m). ✳ Turn R, up round outside fields to the forking tracks at the corner of Blackheath Common (200m).

ⓒ *Short cut of 900m/¾ mile: Fork R steeply up over the rise to the 5-way junction at the corner of the fence (200m). Take the path ½R down to Littleford Lane (250m). Follow the path through the car park down to the first crossing path (150m). Turn R.* ♦⑨

⑤ Fork L (10m) and bear R up the oblique path (150m). Turn R up the steeper side path to the top. Cross the two ridge paths to the road (200m) and go on to the L bend before a slight mound (100m).

⑥ Turn L and pass L of the cricket pitch to the houses (200m).

⑦ Go L on the track (40m) and R between gardens to the road (40m). ☆✳ Walk up the road R and into the village car park (150m). ✧

⑧ At the cross path halfway along the car park go R (S) to the 6-way junction (250m). Stay ahead on the middle path and drop to the straight cross path in the trees (250m).

⑨ Carry on over a bridleway (30m) and Hallams gravel drive (20m) to the brow of the hill (50m) and down to the road (150m). Walk down the road L past Hallams Farm to the next drive (300m). Turn L.

⑩ Go along Darbyn's Brook drive (300m). Curve R across the end of the pond and L up past the house (100m). At the end of the tarmac go R up the track to the road (250m).

⑪ Walk down the road R into the valley and up to the house L near the top, Blackmoor Lodge (350m).

⑫ Beside the drive, take the footpath up between fields to the top of the ridge (400m) and turn L along the winding ridge path, passing the farm entrance (300m). ✧ ↘↗ (North Downs far L; South Downs far R)

⑬ At the barns L, turn R down the hill (100m). Go L round a U-bend and on down to the road (500m).

⑭ Slightly L (30m) take the drive up around the houses and along the straight section (300m). ✦

⑮ Enter the first field L, at the drive L, but keep on in the same direction beside the hedge down to the bottom corner (250m) and between gardens to Shamley Green (150m). The **Bricklayers Arms** is L (50m). The **Red Lion** is 100m ahead over the green.

33 Shamley Green to Winterfold Hill

About 8.5 km/5¼ miles with an extension of 900m/½ mile and an alternative section. Hilly Greensand woods; fine but brief vistas; boggy bits; soft sand in summer. OS maps 1:25000 145 Guildford, 1:50000 186 Aldershot +187 Dorking.

Start near Shamley Green crossroads. Park beside Woodhill Lane, TQ 032 438. Avoid parking near the cricket green if play may start. Alternatively start from Winterfold Hill car park (Hurtwood Control 5), TQ 058 426.

Linking 30✿ 32✧ 34✪ 37✼ ⟨37⟩✦ ⟨39⟩✦

The Bricklayers Arms ☎ 01483 898377
The Red Lion ☎ 01483 892202

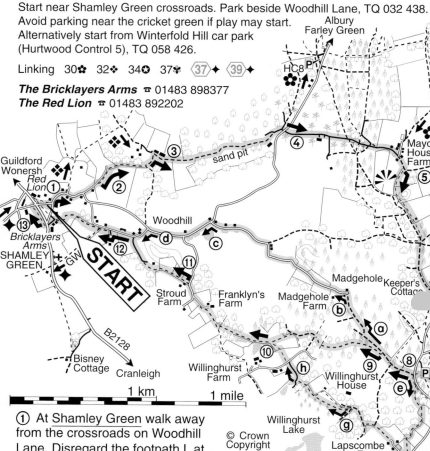

© Crown Copyright MC 100011861

① At Shamley Green walk away from the crossroads on Woodhill Lane. Disregard the footpath L at the 1st R bend (250m) ✿ and go on to the 2nd R bend (150m).

② Bear L up the Shamley Wood drive (120m) then transfer to the path R of the drive. Carry on up (100m) and round R to the corner of the wood (50m). Go through the trees to the path T-junction (200m).

③ Turn L to the top (100m) then follow the ridge track R all the way to the R bend and lane (1000m). ✿

④ Cross the lane. Carry on up the hard track, over the hilltop (500m), down to Mayor House Farm (300m) and ahead up to the L bend (100m).

⑤ Watch out for the side path up R and follow it at the R edge of the fields over the hill (200m) ⬊ and down (250m). After the fields, stay ahead on path & track over a stony cross track (150m) and up (350m).

66

⑥ Join the track from the farm buildings (Keeper's Cottage) and follow it round the bend, up to the road (200m). Continue up the track opposite to the next road (400m). Go on (L) along the road (50m) and R to the car park (60m). ✲❂

⑦ At Winterfold Hill car park (HC5) walk to the brow of the hill then R. Stay on the main path to the next car park: on the edge of the hill, zig zag (150m); then R, almost level, winding about 20m from the brow (300m). Cross the bottom of HC6 car park and continue down to the road (150m). Cross to the track.

ⓔ *Extension of 900m/½ mile: Take the path R of the road (60m), then diverge R from the road down to a field (150m). Cross the R corner and go on round the trees (300m). In the field before the house cross to the bottom corner (150m).*

ⓕ *Go along the drive R (150m). past the houses and down the path between fields (200m). At the end of the pond turn R on the track (200m).*

ⓖ *Enter the plantation L at the R curve. Diverge from or follow the R edge (300m). Continue outside the hedge of the next field and through trees to more ponds (200m).*

ⓗ *Turn R on the track up to the road (200m). Slightly L, go up the path opposite over the brow and across the grass to the gap in the hedge (150m). In the next field aim a bit L for the end of the garden fence (100m). Turn L.* ➜⑩

⑧ Follow the track to the diverging side path L (250m).

ⓐ *Alternative way of equal length: Stay on the track (200m) then turn*

off R along the ridge top and down to Madgehole (400m).

ⓑ *Follow the tarmac drive down the valley around R & L bends to the lane at cottages (700m) and continue to Woodhill (500m).*

ⓒ *At the end, join the busier lane and go L past the ponds to a lane junction (200m) and on towards Shamley Green (250m).*

ⓓ *At the next house L, Reel Hall, turn off up the private road around the houses (100m).* ➜⑫

⑨ Take the diverging path L which winds and undulates down the flank of the hill (500m). Join the track rising steeply from below and carry on up past the field L (200m). Enter the field and descend towards the pond (200m).

⑩ Follow the fence down R of the ponds to the next path junction (350m). Bear R. Carry on to the drive (150m) then L beside it briefly and out to the road (100m). Turn R along the road to the bend (100m).

⑪ Next to Stroud Farm go up the path L to the fields (50m) and along the bottom edge (200m). Keep on along the edge of Cucknells Wood, below the garden, and up the drive from the house (300m). Turn L.

⑫ Walk along the straight section of private road to the field (200m) and ahead on the path in the field. When the Greensand Way turns L across the field,✦ carry on to the bottom corner (200m) and between gardens to Shamley Green (200m).

⑬ Emerging between drives turn L to the **Bricklayers Arms** (50m). Cross the B2128 and turn R along the pavement to the crossroads and cricket green (150m). The **Red Lion** is ½ R over the green.

34 Gomshall and Abinger Roughs

About 8.9 km/5½ miles. A North Downs walk, grassland and woods; steep slopes; grand views. OS maps 1:25000 145 + 146 1:50000 187 Dorking.

Start at Gomshall from the roadside in Queen Street near the A25, TQ 082 478.

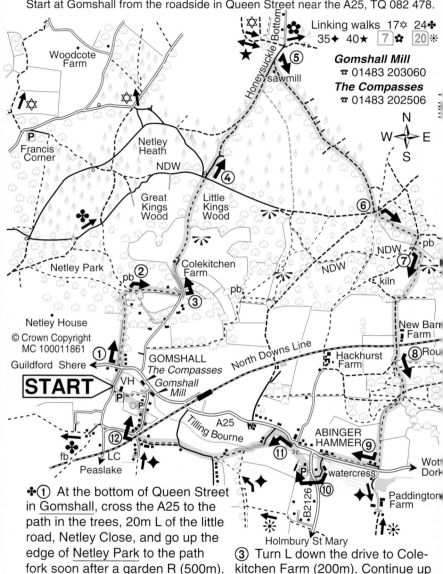

Linking walks 17✿ 24♣ 35✦ 40★ 7 ✿ 20 ☀

Gomshall Mill
☎ 01483 203060
The Compasses
☎ 01483 202506

© Crown Copyright
MC 100011861

♣① At the bottom of Queen Street in Gomshall, cross the A25 to the path in the trees, 20m L of the little road, Netley Close, and go up the edge of Netley Park to the path fork soon after a garden R (500m).
② Bear R, twice, uphill to the path sloping down R (60m). Follow it down past a side path R (10m) and outside a field, to the lane (350m).

③ Turn L down the drive to Colekitchen Farm (200m). Continue up the bridleway past the house ↘↗ to Little Kings Wood (300m) and on through the trees to the major hard track of Netley Heath (300m). ✿

68

④ There are two tracks ahead. Take the R one and stay on it down through Honeysuckle Bottom to the sawmill (900m). ★✿

⑤ Just after the sawmill buildings take the track back R. Disregard all side turns and ascend gently to the major track on top (1300m).

⑥ Go L briefly on the track (20m). Turn R, not on the little side path but on the crosspath. Continue to the next track junction (300m).

⑦ Turn R to the grassland on the brow of the hill (80m). ✳ Turn L into the field (NDW) (50m) ↘↗ then go straight down the hillside, initially towards the nearest farm then to the R end of the bottom hedge (400m). Follow the hedge R (40m) then go down the track L past the farm (350m). Cross the railway and carry on up to the next junction at the top of the fields (80m).

⑧ Turn L on the uphill side track in the trees (Abinger Roughs). Pass over the ridge down to the next cross track (250m). Follow the track R briefly (50m) then diverge L down the side track into the field (60m). Go round the R edge (250m) and on down the sunken path under trees almost to the A25 (250m). ✦

⑨ Turn R up the drive. Continue on the little path above the road, opposite the watercress beds L in the hammer mill pond (400m).

⑩ At the end of the pond take the shop drive L. The wall with water chute R is a hammer mill remnant. Go past the shop and round to the road (150m). Turn R (50m) and go L up the sports club drive. Pass R of the clubhouse and down across the grass and Tilling Bourne footbridge towards the clock (200m).

⑪ Follow the A25 L towards Guildford (200m). Opposite the old farmhouse turn L on the lane and follow it past houses and over the Tilling Bourne (250m). Take the diverging path L up outside the garden to the unmade road with a row of houses (200m). Keep on in the same direction to the R bend in the road (250m). Stay ahead on the path R of the farm track (250m).

⑫ Go under the railway and R on the road to the village green (200m). Either cross the grass and find the path to Queen Street (200m) or go on to **Gomshall Mill** (200m) and L on the A25, past the **Compasses** to Queen Street (250m).

Abinger Hammer Mill, 1557-1787, was the most northerly Wealden iron works, producing 150 tons of wrought iron p.a. Only one wall of it remains. Blooms and pig iron were brought in from bloomeries and blast furnaces elsewhere and heated and beaten to burn off carbon and drive out slag. As well as the hammers, the mill drove bellows, lathes (for gun barrels) and other machinery. Hammer mill ponds had to be large and reliable as hot processing could not be interrupted. This one became the first large-scale watercress farm in Britain in 1850.

From 300BC to the 18th century, the southern edge of Surrey and Sussex were the main area of iron production in Roman and medieval Britain. The richest ore was ironclay nodules from shallow mines in the Weald Clay, the Cretaceous stratum outcropping south of the Greensand. The fuel and reducing agent, charcoal, was kilned from coppiced wood. Iron making declined here after the Midlands iron makers started using coke in 1709.

The Iron Industry of the Weald H Cleere & D Crossley 2nd edition 1995 Merton 425p

35 Gomshall and Sutton Abinger

About 9.2 km/5¾ miles with an extension of 1.7 km/1 mile; farmland with short steep rises, fairly shady. OS maps 1:25000 145 + 146 1:50000 187 Dorking.

Start in Gomshall from the layby at the village green, TQ 084 477.

24✳ 31✿ 34✦ 38✳ 20☆

The Compasses 01483 202506
Gomshall Mill 01483 203060
The Volunteer 01306 730985

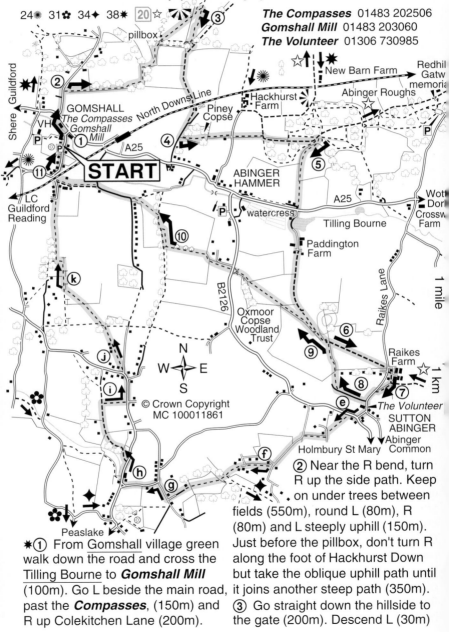

© Crown Copyright MC 100011861

✳① From Gomshall village green walk down the road and cross the Tilling Bourne to **Gomshall Mill** (100m). Go L beside the main road, past the **Compasses**, (150m) and R up Colekitchen Lane (200m).

② Near the R bend, turn R up the side path. Keep on under trees between fields (550m), round L (80m), R (80m) and L steeply uphill (150m). Just before the pillbox, don't turn R along the foot of Hackhurst Down but take the oblique uphill path until it joins another steep path (350m).

③ Go straight down the hillside to the gate (200m). Descend L (30m)

70

and go R down the track, under the railway (400m) and up (200m).

④ On the next descent turn L up through Piney Copse (NT) (200m). Continue ahead at the R edge of the next field (150m), over the lane, along the R edge (200m), up the track into the trees of Abinger Roughs and down to the junction with two side paths R (400m). ☆

⑤ Turn down the 2nd path to the field (60m). Go round the R edge and down the sunken path (450m). Cross the A25 and follow the drive, winding between the fish pond L and hammer mill pond (watercress) R up to Paddington Farm (300m). Slightly L (10m) continue up the track between the gardens. Keep on up between fields over the top to the corner of the field (650m).

⑥ Cross the next field L obliquely towards Raikes Farm (400m).

⑦ Turn R on the road (10m), L into the farm and R on the track between houses (70m). Fork R down the R edge of the field and descend steps to the road (80m). Walk down to the **Volunteer** in Sutton Abinger (200m).

ⓔ *Extension of 1.7 km/1 mile: Stay ahead to the B2126 (80m). Turn R (50m) then L up the steep path between fields to the lane (200m). Continue on the path L of the garden opposite, down to the next lane (150m). Go L up the lane to the junction near houses (300m).*

ⓕ *Just after the side lane R (10m) take the path R (200m). Continue on the tarmac drive, down the path into the valley, ✦ up through trees (200m), up the middle of the next field (200m) and along the path and drive to the lane (200m). ✿*

ⓖ *Turn R on the lane (150m) then L down to the main road (250m).*

ⓗ *Follow the pavement R (200m). then the track L (Broadfield Road) up beside the little valley (350m).*

ⓘ *After the houses L (100m), turn R between fields (200m) and L on the road up to the bend (200m).*

ⓙ *On the crest turn R on Wonham Way. Almost immediately (20m), take the path diverging L between gardens (350m). At the fields turn L briefly down the path at the edge then branch R obliquely across two fields to the hedge (350m).*

ⓚ *Outside the field, follow the path R (200m), round L & R bends and down to Gomshall (500m). ➔⑪*

⑧ Backtrack (50m) and turn up the steep track above the pub (250m). Bear R beside the end garden and keep on along the edge of the field to the track at the corner (500m).

⑨ Go L round outside the R field, watching out for a side turn L (100m). Follow the diverging path down to the road (700m). Opposite, go up the R edge of the field, round the corner of the garden on top (200m) and over the next field past the isolated trees (300m).

⑩ Turn R down the edge (150m) Watch out for access to the sunken path L (150m) and go down that watching out for an oblique side path L (70m). Follow the path across to the end of the line of houses and out (200m). Go round the bend in the unmade road and keep on along it (250m). At the R bend, stay ahead on the path R of the farm track past the farm (250m).

⑪ Pass under the railway ☀ and R down the road to the village green (200m).

36 Peaslake, Pitch Hill and Winterfold Forest

About 7.3 km/4½ miles with an extension to Winterfold Hill of 2.7 km/1⅔ miles.
Short steep slopes on the Lower Greensand; mainly heath and woodland; grand
views. OS maps 1:25000 145 Guildford, 1:50000 187 Dorking.

Start from Peaslake car park, behind the Hurtwood Inn, TQ 086 448, or Pitch Hill
car park (HC3), TQ 079 426, or, on the extension, Winterfold Hill car park
(HC5), TQ 063 427. Several other Hurtwood Control car parks are on the route.

Hurtwood Inn ☎ 01306 730769   Linking walks 30✳ 31☆ 33⊙ 37☆ 39✳
Windmill Inn ☎ 01483 548389   © Crown Copyright MC 100011861

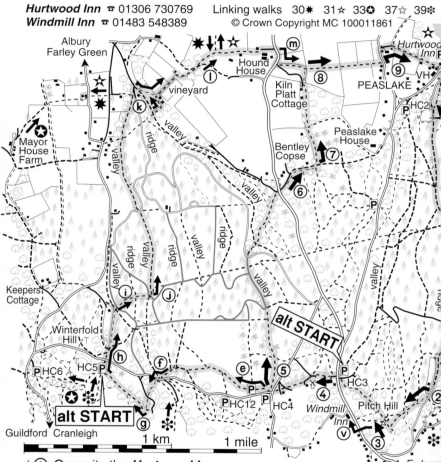

© Crown Copyright MC 100011861

☆① Opposite the **Hurtwood Inn**,
Peaslake, go up the drive past the
church (80m). At the R curve, stay
ahead up the path to the hard track
L of the cemetery (350m). Keep on
to the fork (700m) then bear L up
the edge of Pitch Hill to the tarmac
drive at the house R (1300m). ✻

② After the garden turn R up the
winding path to the top (100m). Go
L on the edge of the escarpment
(100m). Fork L along the brow of
the hill to the view point (100m).
Turn R up to the trig point (80m).

ⓥ *To visit the* **Windmill Inn** *drop down the steep path next to the trig point (250m). After the pub go up the road (300m).* ➘④

③ Keep to the main path past the trig point along the edge of the hill soon winding down to the car park, Hurtwood Control HC3 (500m).

④ Opposite the car park exit go up the drive of Mill Cottage and ahead on the path to the top of the slope (100m). Carry on along the house drive and bear L on the branch drive past the windmill and the next house (150m). Stay ahead down to the nasty road junction (200m).

ⓔ *Extension of 2.7 km/1⅔ miles to Winterfold Hill: From the road opposite take the diverging path R, past car park HC12 (150m) then curving R (350m). Avoid the R fork and keep on to the 3-way junction on the edge of the slope (200m).*

ⓕ *Bear L down to the road (100m). Slightly R (20m), immediately after the path in the cleft, go up through the trees, over the knoll and across the drive, down to the path (200m).*

ⓖ *Turn R along the brow path to the next car park (400m).* ✪

ⓗ *At Winterfold Hill car park, HC5, walk away from the brow of the hill, (60m), over the road and ahead to the fork and fence (80m). Skirt R of the fence to the house (250m).*

ⓘ *At the oblique path junction find the uphill side path opposite the house. Ascend, over a track, to the top of the ridge and continue down into the next valley (250m).*

ⓙ *Cross the forestry track and go down the valley track (600m), over a winding tarmac forest drive, past the little ponds. Stay ahead to the drive near a house R (900m).* ✳❋

ⓚ *At the drive bend turn back R below the garden (35m). If possible take the unoffical oblique path up the L field to the top middle (150m). If not, go on to the end of the field (200m), up the path outside it (60m) and back along the top. Enter the field above and follow the L edge past the vineyard to the end (250m). Outside, turn R down to the bridleway in the valley (150m).*

ⓛ *Fork L up to the path junction (150m). ✦ Stay ahead to the house L (300m) and along the drive to the road at* Hound House *(100m).*

ⓜ *Go R on the road (100m). After the curve enter the L field. Follow the L edge into the dip (200m).* ➘⑧

⑤ Cross to the road opposite and immediately turn R at right angles on the descending path into the valley (550m). Stay ahead down the forest track (450m), across tarmac forest road, past ponds L, to a 4-way junction (100m) and over the rise to the road (400m).

⑥ Go up the drive opposite and diverge onto the path R of it. Keep on, parallel with the main track, past the camp site, to the cross path in a dip with a boundary mound (300m).

⑦ Turn L down to the corner of the boundary mound near a field (300m). Slightly R (10m) continue down through the beech wood to the houses and field (600m). Cross to the bottom edge (100m). Turn R.

⑧ Keep on along the fields and the track to the next road (750m).

⑨ Turn L on the road (100m) and R up the drive of Quaker's Orchard. Skirt the garden ahead, go along the R edge of the field and descend beside gardens to the *Hurtwood Inn* in Peaslake (400m).

37 Peaslake, Holmbury Hill and Pitch Hill

About 9 km/5²/₃ miles, mainly through woods; splendid views from the hilltops. Two short very steep ascents. The extension of 600 km/¹/₃ mile, has breakneck paths. OS maps 1:25000 145 Guildford +146 Dorking, 1:50000 187 Dorking.

Start from Peaslake car park (behind the *Hurtwood Inn*), TQ 086 448, or Pitch Hill car park (HC1), TQ 079 426, or Holmbury Hill car park (HC3), TQ 098 431.

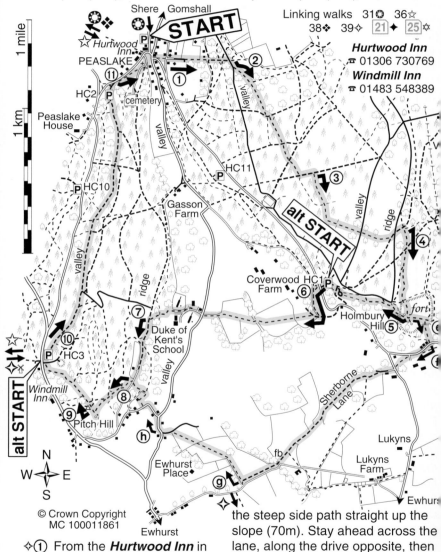

Linking walks 31❁ 36☆
38❖ 39◇ 21◆ 25✿

Hurtwood Inn
☎ 01306 730769

Windmill Inn
☎ 01483 548389

© Crown Copyright
MC 100011861

◈① From the ***Hurtwood Inn*** in Peaslake, cross the main road R of the war memorial (50m), and go up Radnor Road a bit (20m). Turn L on the steep side path straight up the slope (70m). Stay ahead across the lane, along the drive opposite, then track, then footpath under trees (300m) and down through the wood into the valley (150m). Turn R.

② Go up the valley (50m). Fork L up the flank to a track bend (400m). Curve up L (20m) then continue on the brow of the little valley (200m). Cross the winding track (100m) and the oblique track (100m). Turn L on the undulating track (100m).✦

③ Take the next side path R (350m). Go up round a L bend and down to the big forest track in the valley (250m). Carry on over the ridge to the next track (200m) and _ to another big forest track (40m). Cross obliquely and go on to the lesser cross track (80m). ✿

④ Turn R then stay ahead to the cross path on the Holmbury Hill summit (600m) above the Bray memorial seat and view point. ↘

ⓔ Extension of 600m/⅓ mile: Turn L across the end of the hill (100m). Just before the path bends L at the the ramparts, turn R down the breakneck path to the road (150m).

ⓕ Go R past the houses and wall to the drive L (150m). Take the path beside it to the next road (100m). Turn L (15m) & R down the drive (50m), past the house and up the bridleway in the trees, over the hill (150m), past a side path L, down between fields (850m) over the stream then R of the farm road to the end of the long field (300m). ✧

ⓖ Turn R up the edge of the field (200m) then bear L to the gate 80m R of the top corner (250m). Cross the next field to the top L corner (200m) and go L to the road (70m).

ⓗ Turn R up the road (100m) and L up the side road (100m). After the bend (30m) take the path up R and round a bend (100m) then turn L up the breakneck side path to the tarmac drive (100m). Cross it. ✦⑧

⑤ Turn R through the ramparts and carry on at the edge of the hill (250m). When the path bends R to a parallel track, stay ahead on the footpath down to Holmbury Hill car park (Hurtwood Control 1) (300m).

⑥ From the vehicle exit cross the road and go down the L path opposite. Join the bridleway down L to the cart track at the fields (200m). Go R on the track briefly (40m) then bear L on the footpath between the fields. Stay on this path, down, up, down, to the next road (800m). Cross and walk up the drive of the Duke of Kent's School (100m). When it curves L diverge on the tarmac path up past the sports field. Continue on the path into the wood, round a ½L bend and zigzag up the steep slope to the wide track on top (350m).

⑦ Follow the forest track L above the valley to the house (350m). Keep on along the tarmac drive to the end of the garden (100m).

⑧ Go up the winding side path (100m). On top follow the wider path L along the edge of the Pitch Hill escarpment (100m). Fork L on the brow to the view point (100m).

⑨ Turn back R up to the trig point (50m). (**Windmill Inn** down steep path L.) Keep to the L edge of the hill down, past a Hythe Sands quarry R, to the car park (500m). ☆

⑩ Walk down through the car park (HC3). Stay on the valley track all the way to the next car park (HC2) and through it. Fork R on the exit track to the road (2000m).

⑪ Just down from the track, take the little path R up the flank (200m) and go L down the cemetery drive to the *Hurtwood Inn* (150m). ✪

38 Peaslake, Holmbury St Mary and Hill

About 9.0 km/5½ miles, mainly in trees; short steep slopes; a splendid view from Holmbury Hill. OS maps 1:25000 145 + 146 Dorking, 1:50000 187 Dorking.

Start from Peaslake car park (behind the Hurtwood Inn), TQ 086 448, or from Holmbury Hill car park (Hurtwood Control 1), TQ 098 431, or from Holmbury St Mary at the kerbside near the village hall, TQ 107 442, or the *Royal Oak*.

Linking walks
31★ 35✳ 37❖ 21✳ 25❀

The Hurtwood Inn ☎ 01306 730769
The Royal Oak ☎ 01306 898010
The King's Head ☎ 01306 731112

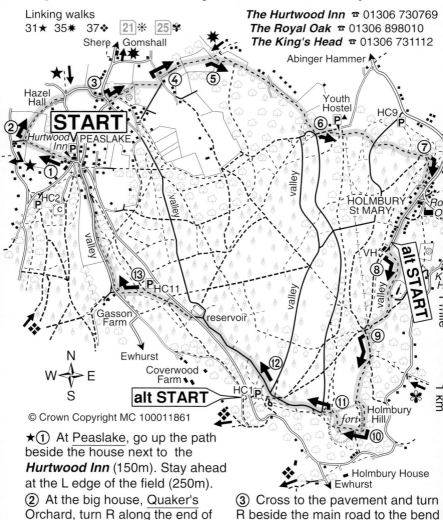

© Crown Copyright MC 100011861

★① At <u>Peaslake</u>, go up the path beside the house next to the *Hurtwood Inn* (150m). Stay ahead at the L edge of the field (250m).

② At the big house, <u>Quaker's Orchard</u>, turn R along the end of the adjacent field (200m). Keep on beside the R hedge in the next field to the road (200m). Turn L (30m), then R down the side lane, Burchets Hollow (300m). ✳

③ Cross to the pavement and turn R beside the main road to the bend (50m). At the lane junction go L up the stepped path (50m). Stay ahead at the L edge of the playing field then bear R between fields (350m) and L up to the road (10m).

④ Turn L (30m) and R up the side lane. Continue on the track then path into the field (200m). Aim for the middle of the far edge (200m).

⑤ Outside, turn R, soon dropping into a valley (80m). Turn R up the valley, beside the wood (150m) then under the trees. Continue up up the edge of the wood (200m), over the lane from the houses, into a little dip (350m) and up to the level track junction (100m).

⑥ Follow the L track (100m). Bear R to skirt the car park (100m) and stay ahead down to the forest track in the valley (200m). Carry on over the ridge to the descent (400m).

⑦ Over the brow, on the R bend, fork L (ahead) on the steeper path curving R down to the road in Holmbury St Mary (200m). ❖※ Go up the side road, Felday Glade, R of the ***Royal Oak*** (100m). Carry on to the village hall (400m).

⑧ Fork L and take the uphill path, opposite the village hall, curving R to the top (250m). Skirt R of the cricket ground and converge on the vehicle track. Continue on the track (R) to the 5-way junction (350m).

⑨ Turn L along the almost level track (200m). After a slight curve, fork R. Keep to the edge of Holmbury Hill, into a dip and on beside the ramparts (500m). ❖

⑩ Go R round the corner of the hill and along the brow to the Bray memorial seat and view point (150m). ↘↗ Go back up the slope to the crosspath (40m) and follow the track away from the edge to the side track L at the uneven ground (N ramparts of fort) (100m).

⑪ Turn L on the track to the next junction (70m). Stay ahead down the main track to a low point (350m) (where paths diverge L to Holmbury Hill (HC1) car park). ❖

⑫ Keep to the main track swinging R up over a rise (200m) and down to the reservoir (550m). Bear L to the road (50m). Cross and go down the track L of the road, past a track converging L (170m) to the steep ½L side path (200m).

⑬ Go down the steep valley side (200m) then follow the small path R, above the road, to a house (600m). Continue down the valley road and L verge to the *Hurtwood Inn* (400m).

North Downs N — Tilling Bourne — Chalk — Folkestone Sands — Bargate — Atherfield Clay — S — Hythe Sands — Weald Clay — Holmbury Hill — Jurassic

Holmbury, Pitch, Leith and Winterfold Hills are the Hythe Sands escarpment of the Lower Greensand, cut into a line of peaks by N-S valleys. The grey rock on the surface occurs as jointed layers of stone in unlithified sand and is quarried for local buildings. Further down the slope brown Bargate used to be quarried; it predominates in the old houses of Holmbury St Mary.

The steepness of the escarpment and valley sides is remarkable. Springs over the edges of the Atherfield Clay undermine the sands and cut back to form valleys. The area has low rainfall and rain is absorbed by the sand, minimizing run-off; so the sides are not washed down and remain steep.

The land visible to the south is on the Weald Clay. It is dissected by gills and used to be heavily wooded. *Weald* derives from the Saxon for forest. Until hard roads and bridges were built, the area was cut off and thinly populated.

39 Pitch Hill and Ewhurst

About 10 km/6¼ miles with an extension of 1.0 km/²/₃ mile to Winterfold Hill; heath, woodland and farmland; Greensand and Weald Clay; long views; short, steep slopes, bluebells. OS maps 1:25000 145 Guildford, 1:50000 187 Dorking

Start from Pitch Hill car park (HC3), TQ 079 426, or from Ewhurst village hall car park, TQ 091 403, via the churchyard path. On the extension, start from Winterfold Hill car park (HC5), TQ 063 427.

Linking walks 33✻ 36✻ 37◇ 24 ✻

The Bull's Head 01483 277447
Windmill Inn 01483 548389

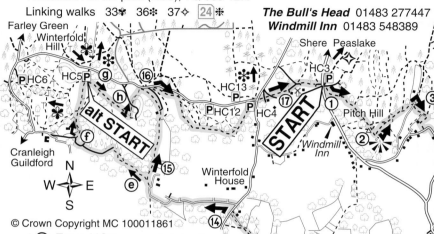

© Crown Copyright MC 100011861

◇① From HC3 car park take the path next to the road up the edge of Pitch Hill to the trig point (450m) and down to the view point (80m).

② Turn back L and follow the path round the end of the hill to a little dip and up on the edge to the L bend (250m). Just before it, bear R down the diverging path and cross the tarmac drive (100m).

③ Descend the steep path to the bottom (100m) and turn R to the road (100m). Walk down the road L, round the R bend to the junction (150m) then down R (100m).

④ Turn L on the next track (70m) and R across the field obliquely to halfway down the R edge (200m). Continue obliquely across the next field to the re-entrant corner (200m) (the castellated house far R is Ewhurst Place) then down the R edge to the tarmac drive (200m).

⑤ Go R on the drive (80m) then take the path L straight over the field to the trees (400m). ✳

⑥ Turn L outside the field to the track (80m), R through trees to the next field (70m) and R round the edge beside the trees (70m). At the corner of the wood carry on beside the ditch to the middle of the field (100m). Turn R along the centre to the re-entrant corner of the wood (130m). Turn L to the hedge (50m) and go on between fields to the drive of Bramblehurst Farm (130m).

⑦ Follow the drive R to the B2127 at the edge of Ewhurst (300m). Cross to the pavement. Turn R (40m) and take the path L between gardens (150m), over a residential road and on to the road (100m).

⑧ Opposite, bear L on Old Rectory Drive (60m) then turn R through the churchyard to the Street (80m).

⑨ Walk along the pavement R to the **Bull's Head** (350m).

⑩ Opposite the pub, go along Wykehurst Lane from the corner of the green, down past houses and up to the wood R (300m). Carry on to the track in the trees R (150m).

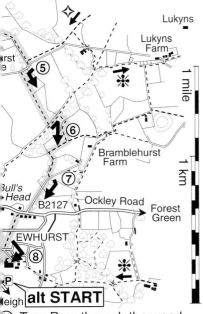

Lukyns
Lukyns Farm
1 mile
rst
⑤
⑥
Bramblehurst Farm
1 km
Bull's Head
⑦
B2127 · Ockley Road
Forest Green
EWHURST
⑧
P
eigh **alt START**

⑪ Turn R up through the wood (100m). Keep on between fields to the farm (400m). Go out R on the winding drive to the road (100m).

⑫ Follow the road L (450m). After the next farm continue on the track (150m), round a R bend past two side paths L near barns R, and on under trees between fields (350m).

⑬ Keep on round the R bend, up through the belt of trees (300m) and over the bridge to the end of the adjacent field R (100m). Join the path on the bank and bear R along the edge of the next field, past a house, to the road (150m).

⑭ Go up the road R (60m) and L along the next drive (450m). At the farm entrance take the drive L round the fields (150m). After the R bend (60m), opposite houses, bear L up the path to the fork (40m).

ⓔ *Extension of 1 km/²⁄₃ mile to Winterfold Hill: Fork L up the side path which winds along the hillside (350m). At the conifer plantation go along the track past another gateway (200m) and round an S-bend to a side path R (70m).*

ⓕ *Follow the steep side path up to the car park (400m). ❋❋ Turn R.*

ⓖ *From Winterfold Hill car park, HC5, take the path SE along the edge of the hill (400m).*

ⓗ *Watch out for a little knoll L. Take the side path over it and down to the road (150m). ➔⑯*

⑮ Fork R then stay ahead up the valley (Jelleys Hollow) between the wood and fields (500m), over a house drive to the road (200m).

⑯ Go R on the verge, past the downhill tracks (70m), then bear R on the rising path beside the road (150m). Fork R then keep to paths and tracks nearest the edge of the hill (450m). Eventually go round the corner of the hill to a car park HC4 and the road junction (300m). ❋

⑰ Go up the path opposite (300m). After the windmill bear R on the drive of the next house and drop down the path to the road opposite Pitch Hill car park, HC3 (150m).

40 West Horsley, Place Farm and Sheepleas

About 7.5 km/4²/₃ miles with a woodland extension of 1.3 km/¾ mile. Farmland and bluebell woods. OS maps 1:25000 145 Guildford, 1:50000 187 Dorking.

Start at the Sheepleas car park, TQ 088 525, behind West Horsley Church or at East Horsley Village Hall, TQ 099 542. The other two Sheepleas car parks are close to the walk route.

Linking walks 17☆ 39★ 41✹ 7

The Barley Mow ☎ 01483 282693

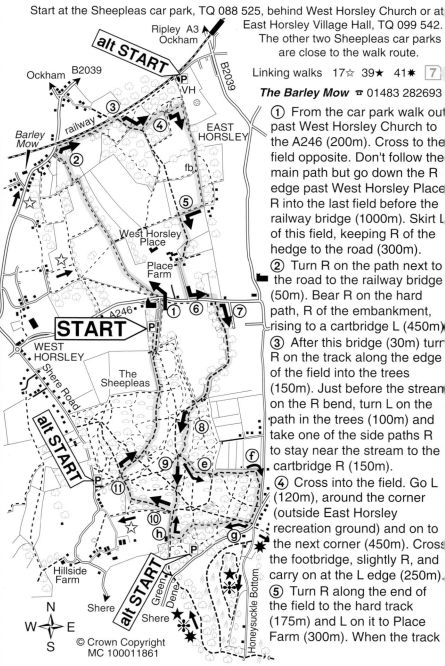

① From the car park walk out past West Horsley Church to the A246 (200m). Cross to the field opposite. Don't follow the main path but go down the R edge past West Horsley Place R into the last field before the railway bridge (1000m). Skirt L of this field, keeping R of the hedge to the road (300m).

② Turn R on the path next to the road to the railway bridge (50m). Bear R on the hard path, R of the embankment, rising to a cartbridge L (450m).

③ After this bridge (30m) turn R on the track along the edge of the field into the trees (150m). Just before the stream on the R bend, turn L on the path in the trees (100m) and take one of the side paths R to stay near the stream to the cartbridge R (150m).

④ Cross into the field. Go L (120m), around the corner (outside East Horsley recreation ground) and on to the next corner (450m). Cross the footbridge, slightly R, and carry on at the L edge (250m).

⑤ Turn R along the end of the field to the hard track (175m) and L on it to Place Farm (300m). When the track

© Crown Copyright
MC 100011861

turns into the yard, pass L of the little barn to the tarmac drive (50m) and walk out to the A246 (250m).

⑥ Follow the pavement L (200m).

⑦ After the house R, cross to the Sheepleas track in the trees. Follow it up to the wood (800m).

⑧ Just after the top of the R field, opposite a path R, there are two side paths L, 10m apart. Turn L on the 2nd one, curving up R. Keep on to the complex junction (400m).

ⓔ *Extension of 1.3 km/¾ mile in the wood: Take the wide path L to fields (300m). Carry on outside the fields over the hilltop (100m).*

ⓕ *Soon after the highest point, fork L down the winding path near the field (150m). Curve R with it and keep on just above the road (200m). Cross the uphill path from the first road junction and go on to the 2nd road junction (150m).* ★✹❋

ⓖ *Turn R up the track from the road (100m) then diverge L on the side path through the yew avenue (300m). At the end, bear L, almost level, to the side path R with a barn visible above (100m).*

ⓗ *Ascend towards the barn (80m) and turn R on the track outside the field (200m).* ➔⑩

⑨ Bear L up the steepest track to the corner of the field R (400m).

⑩ Turn down the side track just below the field (300m). Carry on round the R bend, down to the end of the L field (150m) where there are two paths R opposite one path L (from Shere Road car park).

⑪ Take the 2nd R (church path) past the view point R (200m) and down to the end (750m). Cross the track from the L field and continue under trees to the car park (100m).

Horsley first appears as Horsalæge in the will of a Saxon earl, Elfrede, c880. Part of it was given to the Archbishop of Canterbury in 1032 so there are two ORSELEIs in the Domesday Book, both in the Hundred of Woking.

West Horsley's Saxon lord was Brixi. After the Conquest it went to Walter FitzOther whose family became the Windsor castellans and took the name de Windsor. Henry VIII confiscated the manor in payment of debts and gave it (with E Clandon and other land) to Sir Anthony Browne, captain of the bodyguard & guardian of his children Edward and Elizabeth. His son, also Walter, became 1st Lord Montague and lived at Henley Park. Sir Walter Raleigh's son, Carew,, inherited the manor and lived there with his mother who kept Sir Walter's head in a bag.

West Horsley church, St Mary's, has Saxon foundations of around 1030. The nave walls are Norman, later pierced for the addition of the aisles. Points of interest: tower about 1120; wall paintings about 1200; coffin in the wall near the altar, probably of Hugh de Windsor d.1220; parish chest about 1220; roof timbers about 1300; N window of the chancel with portrait of Sir James de Berners (beheaded 1388) in old Chiddingfold glass; the recessed 14th century tomb of a priest, probably Ralph de Berners. Sir Walter Raleigh's head is buried under the floor. Church house, next door, has timbers dated to 1434.

The History of West Horsley, Church & Village S Aston 1974 141pp

West Horsley Place is a very ancient manor house built around a hall of the 14th century. Much of it is Tudor timber-frame work made fashionable by a brick façade around 1650.

East Horsley in the Domesday Book was held by Archbishop Lanfranc of Canterbury for support of the monks. They retained it until the Dissolution. The grand house, Horsley Towers, at the bend in the A246 was built for Lord Lovelace who bought the manor in 1829. He already owned Ockham.

41 Sheepleas and the Lovelace Arches

About 9 km/5½ miles with a short cut of 1.7 km/1 mile; forest and farmland, steep slopes, bluebells. OS maps 1:25000 145 +146, 1:50000 187 Dorking.

Start at Shere Road Sheepleas car park, TQ 084 514. Green Dene Sheepleas car park, TQ 091 509, is near the route

Linking walks
17✻ 40✷ 7✦ 8✧

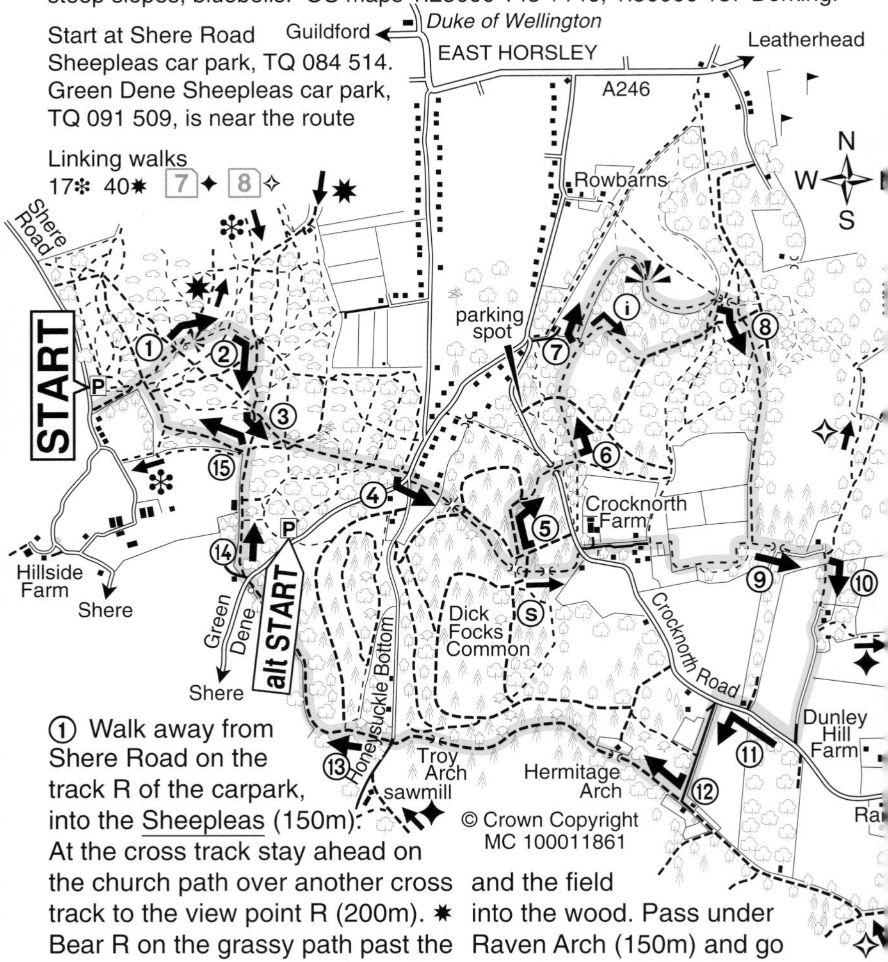

Guildford
Duke of Wellington
EAST HORSLEY
Leatherhead
A246
N
W
S
Rowbarns
Shere Road
START
parking spot
Crocknorth Farm
Hillside Farm
Shere
Green Dene
alt START
Honeysuckle Bottom
Dick Focks Common
Crocknorth Road
Dunley Hill Farm
Troy Arch
sawmill
Hermitage Arch
Ra
© Crown Copyright MC 100011861

① Walk away from Shere Road on the track R of the carpark, into the Sheepleas (150m). At the cross track stay ahead on the church path over another cross track to the view point R (200m). ✷ Bear R on the grassy path past the view point into the valley (200m).

② Go up the path opposite to the track junction (100m) and turn R up the main (& steepest) track to the oblique crossing bridleway (250m).

③ Bear L up this. At the junction on top (150m), stay ahead down through the trees into Green Dene (400m). Cross the road to the lane.

④ Just into the lane, take the bridleway up L between the drive and the field into the wood. Pass under Raven Arch (150m) and go on to Briary Hill Arch W (300m).

ⓢ *Short cut of 1.7 km/1 mile: Stay ahead under the next arch up to the road (250m), along the drive of Crocknorth Farm opposite, past houses (250m) then on the path between fields (80m). Now make for the forest at the far side of the fields: Go round the R edge of the fields to the path junction at the corner of the forest (400m).* ➔⑨

⑤ Just after the arch, and 60m before the next one, go L on the track (50m) then L & R (20m) and along the brow of the hill (200m) until round the R bend (40m). On the L curve take the side path R to the road-cutting (150m). Cross the Dorking (Lovelace) Bridge and go on to the major cross path (70m).

⑥ Turn L down the slope (200m) Cross the forest track (140m R of the road and parking spot, out of sight). Keep on down into the dry valley and up. Watch out for the path L before the corner of a field visible through the trees (200m).

⑦ The best route is in the field but there is no public right of way and the path may get closed. Turn L into the field. Follow the path up the R edge to the corner of the wood (300m), round R still near the wood. ↘ Behind, Horsley Towers is visible. Keep on to the public path in the dip (400m). Turn R into the wood to Stony Dene Arch. ⟶⑧

ⓘ *If the field path is closed, carry on up round the R bend and across the top of the hill to a major forest track (250m). Turn L down this track (200m). Between slight L & R bends at the bottom, turn L on the cross path near the field to Stoney Dene Arch (100m).*

⑧ Walk under the arch, away from the field, to the next cross path (50m) and turn R up the slight slope. Stay ahead over the top (500m) and ahead beside fields to the corner of the forest L (350m).

⑨ Follow the path away from the corner of the field along the end of the forest and under Meadow Plat Arch to the tarmac drive (120m). Descend past the house (120m). ✦

⑩ Turn R on the path at the edge of the wood (200m). Stay ahead past two houses on the tarmac drive, ✦ over the rise, down and up to Crocknorth Road (450m).

⑪ Walk along the road R past the wood into the dip with a house R (200m) and up to the forest track L (100m). Follow the forest track to the T-junction near a house (350m).

⑫ Turn R on the byway through the forest. Keep to the track down through Hermitage Arch (300m) and Troy Arch (650m) to the tarmac at Honeysuckle Bottom near the sawmill (150m).

⑬ Stay ahead up the path steeply (100m), then level, round a R curve and down to Green Dene (700m).

⑭ Continue ahead up the path opposite, over the hill and on beside the field L (450m). ❋

⑮ Just after the field turn L down the track (300m). Pass round the R bend (200m) and take the next L to Shere Road car park (150m).

The **Lovelace Arches** were built in the 1860s for William King, 1st Earl Lovelace, it is said, for forestry carts to cross existing byways. There were 15 arches initially but only 10 survive, restored in recent times. Their arches are usually horseshoe-shaped with brick and flint masonry, but in a great variety of sizes, 6 - 18' wide.

Earl Lovelace owned East Horsley and Ockham manors where flint and ornate brickwork are features of the estate houses. He lived at the Gothic mansion, Horsley Towers. Originally East Horsley Park, it was built by Sir Charles Barry for William Currie. Earl Lovelace enlarged it and added the towers in the 1830s. Ada, Lady Lovelace, Byron's daughter, invented machine algorithms in 1843. Tommy Sopwith later lived there.

42 Great Ridings Wood and Effingham Common

About 8.5 km/5¼ miles. An extension of 900m/¾ mile & short cut of 1 km/²/₃ mile can be combined. Farmland and woods on the London Clay, slightly undulating; summer shade. OS maps 1:25000 146 Dorking, 1:50000 187 Dorking.

Start from the Effingham sports club car park off Browns Lane, TQ 119 534.
If linking to Walk 44, start from the kerbside in Orestan Road, TQ 108 535,
or from Effingham Common cricket ground car park, TQ 105 552.

Linking walks   43✳   44☆

The Sir Douglas Haig ☎ 01372 456886
The Plough ☎ 01372 458121

Village Logo Ark Royal I
Lord Howard's flagship

① At the clubhouse of Effingham Sports Club take the tarmac path towards the trees (100m). Continue through the trees to the path at the far edge (100m) then turn L (100m).

② Cross the churchyard to the far L corner (50m) and go down Crossways opposite to The Street (100m). Cross slightly L and take the drive past the end of the shops. Keep on to the first field R (100m).

③ Cross the field on the diagonal footpath (250m). Continue in the same direction to the road (300m). Go L on the pavement (350m).

④ At the end of Orestan Road, continue on the track into the wood. Stay on the track over the rise to the junction at the flint wall (350m).

84

⑤ Follow the wall down R (200m). When it bends L, fork R on the path through Great Ridings Wood to the road with houses (800m).

⑥ Cross the road into Effingham Common. Follow the R edge past a house R (450m) & sheds (100m).

⑦ After the sheds follow the path curving L over the grass, R of two clumps of trees at ponds, to the ditch (200m). Cross ✻ and turn R.

ⓔ *Extension of 900m/¾ mile: Follow paths around the L edge of the grass near the fringe of trees, all the way to the road near Effingham Junction (850m).*

ⓕ *Cross into the drive opposite (50m) and take the side path R through the wood (400m). Bear R on the track outside the wood past the farm buildings (300m).*

ⓖ *At the drive, turn R to the Common (40m) and L along the edge (150m). ➧⑨*

⑧ Follow paths along the trees fringing the R edge of the grass (300m). Turn R across the end of the cricket field (150m) and go L on the drive (150m). Cross the road and take the oblique path over the grass, R of the drive (200m).

⑨ Turn L along the road to the far end (450m) and enter the field.

ⓢ *Short cut of 1 km/⅔ mile: Walk down the R edge (80m) and cross the corner to the gate (80m). Go out, over the bridge and over the drive to the next field (80m). Cross the L corner and follow the L edge (200m). At the corner of the pond fence, bear L in a straight line across the curve to the gate at the L corner (200m). Pass the water into the next field (40m) and cross obliquely to the top corner (150m).*

ⓣ *In the field above turn L along the fence to the end (100m). Go R, along the track, outside the fields, round L & R curves (300m). ➧⑭*

⑩ Follow the cart track L (100m), round the corner R and on until it bends L (400m). Stay ahead through the fields near the L hedge and ditch (350m). In the field before the farm, turn L over the footbridge to the L edge (50m) and go up the railway fence to the track from the railway bridge (300m).

⑪ Turn R (50m). Cross the road and follow the path R of it (250m).

⑫ Just before the road bends L, take the path R between gardens (100m). Cross a road and follow the drive opposite (100m). When it bends into the end garden, turn L along the path between gardens to the first field L (200m)

⑬ At the cross path from the field bear R through the wood (200m) then L on the track out to fields (30m). Turn L on the major track.

⑭ Go round to the end of the wood (100m) and stay on the same track, between fields, all the way down to houses (600m).

⑮ At the junction of drives with the tarmac road look for the path R between hedges. Follow it to the road (250m). Cross slightly R (20m) and continue to the cross path between Little Bookham Church L and the school R (100m). ✸ Turn R.

⑯ If returning to Effingham sports club bear L on the side path along the boundary to open grass (250m) and cross R (300m). If not stay ahead past the school to Effingham churchyard (450m). ➧②

Barnes Wallis' grave is near the south edge with modern headstone.

43 Bookham and Effingham Commons

About 9.2 km/5¾ miles with a short cut of 2.4 km/1½ miles; farmland and woods on the London Clay, gently undulating, muddy and slippery in wet seasons. OS maps 1:25000 146 Dorking, 1:50000 187 Dorking.

Start from Plains car park (NT/free), Bookham Common, TQ 125 558. There are free NT car parks at Hundred Pound Bridge (via Downside), TQ 120 567, and Mark Oak, TQ 133 568. Effingham Common car park (NT/pay), TQ 105 552, is nearby.

Linking walk 42❄

Olde Windsor Castle 01372 452226

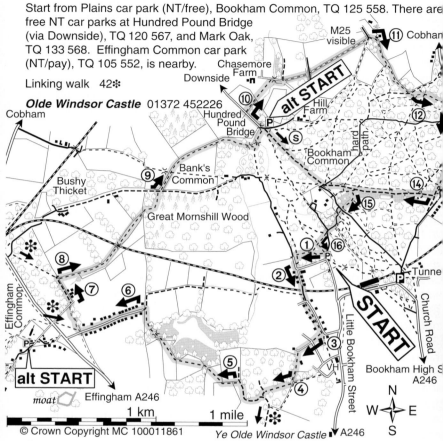

© Crown Copyright MC 100011861

① From Plains car park, pass the cattle grid and immediately take the side path L and fork L through the trees parallel with the (hidden) road to a T-junction at the edge of Bookham Common (200m).

② Turn L & R to the lane (50m). Go L to the L bend (40m), ahead on the smaller lane and over the railway bridge to the next road (250m). Cross and follow the path ahead, R of the road (250m).

③ Just before the road bends L, take the path R between gardens (100m). Cross a residential road and follow the drive opposite (100m). When it bends into the end garden, turn L on the path between gardens to the first field L (200m).

④ At the cross path from the field bear R through the wood (200m) and L, at the end, to fields (40m). ❄ Follow the track R, winding round the edge of the wood (250m).

⑤ When the track enters the field follow the path L outside this field (120m) and turn R into the corner of the next adjacent field. Cross diagonally to the corner at the wood (120m) and go through the trees past the corner of the pond to the next field (50m). Cut across the bulge of the R edge to the end of the trees (200m) then follow the R edge and go straight on over to the L corner (200m). Outside the field, cross the drive and the pond dam up to the next field (80m). Ascend across the L corner and go up the L edge to the road (150m).

⑥ Follow the road (450m). After the houses turn R along the edge of Effingham Common to the farm drive (200m).

⑦ Turn R, away from the green, (40m) then L on the path at the edge of the wood, past the farm buildings to the first field R (200m).

⑧ Take the path R between hedges (150m). Go on along the narrow field (350m), under the railway, between fields (300m) and through the wood round a L bend (100m) to the track (100m).

⑨ Slightly R (20m), continue on the other side, between fields (500m). After the R field carry on through scrub and over a footbridge to the path junction (250m). Turn L over another footbridge to Hundred Pound Bridge and car park (150m).

⑤ *Short cut of 2.4 km/1½ miles: At Hundred Pound Bridge, take the path away from the road in line with it. Keep on to the track junction near buildings (600m). Stay on the same path round the ½L bend (150m). At the next cross path, turn R to the pond.* ➔⑮

⑩ Walk along the road to the end of the wood (100m) and take the path R at the edge of the field (100m). Stay ahead to the farm road (200m). Cross the farm bridge R to the track L along the hedge (60m). Bear slightly L up between paddocks to the hedge on the ridge top (180m). Stay ahead between more paddocks to the top (470m).

⑪ Cross the track to the path in the trees. Pass R of the house (50m) and round the R bend, down the edge of the Common to the end of the fields (400m).

⑫ Turn L, not on the horse track beside the field but on the smaller path diverging above it, winding to a T-junction (100m). Turn R to Sheepbell Pond (70m) and keep on to the cross track just before Mark Oak car park (100m). Turn R.

⑬ Follow the wide hard path in the trees past paths from Mark Oak car park (100m). Don't go round the R bend but stay ahead down to a fork (100m). Fork L on the footpath to the track (350m) and continue ahead to the major junction (50m).

⑭ Follow the path round R to the pond L with bird-hide (100m). Keep on past another pond, past the causeway path L (200m) and past more ponds L (350m). At the next cross path turn L to the pond.

⑮ Follow the broad path L round the pond to the vehicle track behind it (200m). Cross the track and go along the path to the next track (40m). Follow that L, out of the trees, to the track junction (150m).

⑯ Cross the bridge. Immediately take the footpath diverging R of the track to the cross path (100m). Turn L to Plains car park (100m).

44 Effingham and Polesden Lacey

About 8.8 km/5½ miles with an extension of 2.1 km/1⅓ miles around Polesden Lacey. Undulating farm country on the north face of the North Downs. Polesden Lacey can be visited. OS maps 1:25000 146 Dorking 1:50000 187 Dorking.

Start from the Effingham sports field car park off Browns Lane, TQ 119 534, or from Polesden Lacey at North Lodge (free) car park, TQ 135 527.

Linking walks 42★ 1 ✿ 8 ☆ 9 ★

The Sir Douglas Haig 01372 456886
The Plough 01372 458121

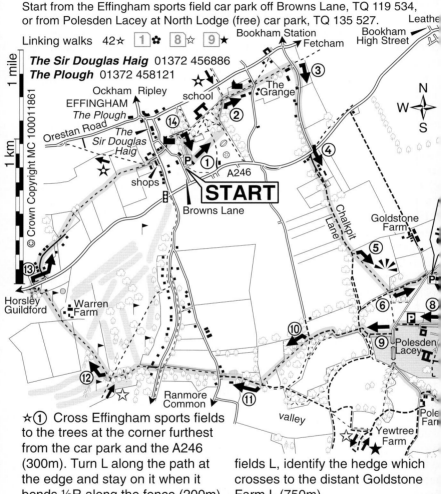

★① Cross Effingham sports fields to the trees at the corner furthest from the car park and the A246 (300m). Turn L along the path at the edge and stay on it when it bends ½R along the fence (200m).

② Bear R on the path from the school passing R of Little Bookham Church to the road (250m). Stay ahead to the next road (300m).

③ Walk up the road R (Rectory Lane) to the A246 (700m).

④ Cross slightly R and walk up Chalkpit Lane, a track. At the open fields L, identify the hedge which crosses to the distant Goldstone Farm L (750m).

⑤ Just after it (10m) enter the field. Identify the top edge and cross diagonally to the L corner (350m).☆

⑥ Outside, follow the track L (300m). ✿ Continue on the farm drive briefly then cut across the car park R and the grass to the North Lodge and main drive (100m).

⑦ Walk along the fence R or L of the drive, almost to the main gates of Polesden Lacey (350m).

ⓔ *Extension of 2¼ km/1⅓ miles around Polesden Lacey: Turn L into the field and follow the R edge (250m). Go round the R bend then diverge slightly from the R edge to the far L corner (200m). Go through gates to the next field (30m) and make your way across to the distant bottom corner (350m). ★ Cross the old carriage drive into the next field and descend to the bottom L corner (200m).*

ⓕ *In the next field turn R along the edge to the wood (350m). Stay ahead: wood, field, wood, field (450m). Just before the farm, continue into the trees and bear L to the tarmac drive (150m). Go up the drive under the garden bridges (400m). Turn L at the field.* →⑨

⑧ Go R, through the NT car park to the far L corner (300m). Outside the car park go round the bend past the house (50m) and turn R.

⑨ Follow the track at the L edge of the field (200m). Just round the end, turn L across the track in the trees and carry on. Keep to the track round the S-bend (200m) but not round the next R bend (150m).

⑩ There are two side paths L from the R bend. Take the 2nd one, through the trees and over the field to the far L corner (450m).

⑪ Turn R on the track outside the field and stay on it to the road (300m). Cross to the field slightly R. Follow the top edge (350m) then bear L through the trees to the road (30m). Cross to the drive opposite and follow the track from it, continuing on the path to the golf course (150m). Bear L across the fairway to the path in the clump of trees (100m). Follow the path in the trees. At the 2nd cross path curve R to the edge (150m).

⑫ Follow the public footpath down the golf course 30m L of the hedge-end. Diverge from the hedge, aiming L of the distant farm; skirt R of the small clump of trees (200m). Continue in the same line down through the next hedge (150m), across the corner with the farm below (150m) and over the grass to the shed in the trees (200m). Follow the path L to the road and cross to the pavement (100m)

⑬ Turn R (20m) then join the path behind the trees (100m). Follow the unmade Salmons Road L, down to the lowest point (350m). At the low point, before the last house, enter the L field and diverge from the R edge to the middle of the top edge, R of the clump of trees (250m). Go on between fields (600m) then along the drive to the Street in Effingham (100m). (Down the road L is the **Sir Douglas Haig** 200m). Slightly L, go up Crossways opposite to the churchyard (80m). Pass round the church and out on lhe sunken path beside the flint wall, before the far L corner (100m).

⑭ In the trees behind the church yard, turn R on one of the side paths to the sports field and cross to the car park (200m).

The **A3** evolved out of the ancient road from London Bridge to Portsmouth via Kingston, Guildford, Godalming and Petersfield which were successively bypassed. Hindhead, the last bottle-neck, was bypassed by tunnel in 2011.

Abinger Hammer had a hammer mill, 1557-1787. Its position on the Tilling and the name of Abinger *Sutton* (south farm) suggest it was the original head of the manor. Darwin experimented on earthworms on the Roman mosaic floor at Abinger Hall (demolished 1959). The blacksmith clock replaced an earlier one in 1909. In the Domesday Book Abinger was ABINCEBORNE. The parish stretches nine miles southwards from the top of the Downs. The church and manor house are 1½ miles away at the village of Abinger Common. Greenwich Observatory had a station at Abinger Bottom that monitored the Earth's magnetic field until the railway was electrified; during World War II it became the bomb-proof broadcast station for the Greenwich time-signal

Albury is ELDEBERIE in Domesday Book. It had a church and mill. The estate belonged to the d'Abernons for 5 centuries but has passed through many families since. The medieval village was near the old church but in the 18th century pressure was put on villagers to move to the present site. A 19th century owner, Henry Drummond, built the new village church in 1842. Residents of note have been Malthus the political economist and Martin Tupper the writer. The estate came to the Dukes of Northumberland through the marriage of Drummond's daughter. The Albury in New South Wales was proclaimed a city in 1946.   *Albury - A short Guide to the Parish* Albury Trust 1994

Albury Catholic Apostolic Church is a fine Victorian Gothic structure built in 1840. Out of social turmoil in the early 19th century arose the desire for a second coming and reform of church practices. A conference at Albury Park in 1826 led to the formation of the new sect. Twelve apostles were chosen to guide it and seven churches were built in London. Drummond, one of the apostles, built the Albury Catholic Apostolic church at the same time as the present village church. No provision was made to replace the apostles and the sect died out; the London churches were sold and Albury Catholic Apostolic church is redundant. *The Years of Ferment* R C Walmsley & G L Standring 1980 Albury Park

Albury Mill was the name for several mills at different times. The one in the middle of the village was owned by John Weston in 1255 and was a flour mill until about 1900. It was burned down in 1830 and James Warner was the last person to be hung for arson.

Albury Old Church was the village church until 1842. There is a hint of herringbone stonework at the foot of the north wall of the Saxon chancel which was reinforced around 1140 to form the tower. The shingled cupola was added in 1820. The chancel is 13th century. The knight-in-armour brass of 1440 in the nave floor is John Weston. The Drummond Chapel is elaborately decorated. Martin Tupper was not interred with Anthony Devis as shown on the white table tomb near the porch.

Albury Park, the Victorian Gothic mansion, became apartments in 1970. John Evelyn designed the garden in 1667; Cobbett rode through in 1822, writing of it as the *prettyest in England*. An Albury mill formerly near the church had a role in European politics. The Comte d'Artois (later Charles X of France) visited in 1893 to get paper made with watermarks for counterfeit banknotes to upset the French Revolution. Later, Russian watermarks were used to upset the Czar.

Artington is now occupied by part of Guildford. The manor was cut off from the great Royal Manor of Godalming by Henry II for Master David around 1171 as a reward for negotiating with Rome after the murder of Thomas Becket. It was appended to the Loseley estate by Sir George More in 1601.

Bargate is the chief building stone of old Guildford and Godalming, medium rown when unsooted. The origin of the name is unknown. Ancient photos of Godalming quarries show men jumping on crowbars to lever out huge *doggers* rom which the building stone was cut. t is a Lower Greensand calcareous sandstone which occurs only here. The oil on it is good enough for cereals. Further east around Holmbury St Mary and Peaslake the stratum outcrops as thin seams of jointed stone, yellower and more crumbly.

Blackheath was BLACHETFELDE in the Domesday Book, not a manor but the name of the hundred. It included Bramley, Chilworth, Shalford, etc. The men of the hundred probably met and held courts in the open on the heath. The present village is small and in the midst of heath. Blackheath Common, currently 108 hectares, is managed by Waverley Borough Council. Part of it is an SSSI. It has been used for army camps from time to time: during the Napoleonic wars and in Victorian times. The Canadian army enclosed it as a camp in World War II.

Blackwell Farm is owned by the University of Surrey and the house is the residence of the Vice Chancellor.

Bookham Common is the commons of Great and Little Bookhams which were given to the National Trust in 1920 with the adjacent Banks Common, totalling 170 ha/370 acres. Historically, land that was uneconomical for cultivation was waste left for communal grazing and timber. London Clay underlies most of the Common but there are patches of residual Ice Age sand and gravel. The ponds were developed for fish farming in the 17th century but the ancient owner, Chertsey Abbey, may well have started them. The Common has been intensely studied by the London Natural History Society since the 1940s.

Bower's Lock is on the original cut of the Wey Navigation which bypassed a ½ mile loop of the river, made about 1620. Bowers Mill closed in 1910 and was demolished in 1945. In 1733 it was insured as a paper and flour mill; in the 1860 OS map it is shown as an oil mill.

Brabhœuf Manor was detached from Artington around 1214 and remained in the same family until 1914. The manor house of 1586 is timber-framed with a stone facade. It is the admin building of the University of Law with classroom blocks clustered around it. This is the HQ with branches in Chester, London, York and Birmingham, providing 1 & 2-year courses for trainee solicitors.

The **Bramley Wey** is a small river, aka Cranleigh Water, in an immense valley, best seen from the hills above Shamley Green and Hascombe. It is aligned with the Guildford notch in the North Downs which suggests it was the parent Wey though smaller than present tributaries. It flows from Vachery Pond to Shalford.

Broadmead on the flood plain of the River Wey was medieval communal land shared between Woking and Send for hay production. Grazing was allowed only from September to March.

Broadstreet Common is scattered patches of grassland and scrub on the London Clay - unlike typical Surrey commons. A Roman house stood here.

The **chalk** pits in the area are all now defunct, often denoted by clumps of trees on hillsides. Chalk was dug as a fertilizer and kilned to make mortar. The lime was needed to treat the sour soils of the adjacent Lower Greensand. Chalk is a limestone which, discounting flints, is often 98% calcium carbonate. It formed on the sea bed as an ooze of coccoliths from planktonic algæ and the shells of microscopic and larger animals probably in an ocean warmer than anywhere at present. The animals that lived in the water and on the bottom became the abundant fossils. Chalk corrodes easily but is sometimes used internally in buildings, eg Compton church pillars, Loseley's fireplaces. A hard chalk, Melbourne Rock, was mined in Guildford.

Chantries Hill is a Lower Greensand ridge with thin seams of bargate stone which give greater fertility and permit grassland instead of heath along the Five Fields. It was given to Holy Trinity

Church, Guildford in 1486 by Henry Norbrigge (mayor, d.1512); there is a brass plate to him near George Abbott's tomb. The rent or produce of a chantry paid for prayers for the soul of the donor or others named by him and was often used to fund an extra curate as schoolmaster for a church school whose pupils chanted the prayers. Chantries were dissolved soon after monasteries by Acts of 1545 & 1547.

Chilworth is CELEORDE in the Domesday Book, a small manor with a mill, owned by Bishop Odo of Bayeux. The present manor house with Dutch gables is a 17th century rebuild by Vincent Randyll, owner of the manor and gunpowder mills, 1653-73 who sold up to the Duchess of Marlborough after the South Sea Bubble.

Chilworth Old Mill is the mill house of Great Chilworth Mill which made paper from about 1700 to 1870. On the same site was the first gunpowder mill of the East India Company but there were wire, fulling and flour mills before it and probably the one taxed @ 7 shillings in the Domesday Book. Nearby was Little Chilworth Mill which burned down in 1895 threatening to ignite the adjacent gunpowder magazine. This was Unwins printing works. They decamped to (Old) Woking Mill (Gresham Mill apartments).

Chinthurst Hill was bought by Surrey County Council in 1961 with financial aid from London County Council to preserve it as a public open space. The eponymous house, now divided, is by Lutyens. The bargate sandstone tower was built as a folly in 1936 but has been used as a house.

East **Clandon** is a nucleated village with some very old cottages, Frogmore Cottage of around 1500 and Tunmore Cottage 1550. The manor was probably part of the original endowment in 675 to Chertsey Abbey who owned it for 800 years. The Domesday Book entry for CLANDVN records that the villeins held it from the abbey without a lord of the manor. It appears to show a tax-fiddle by Odo, Bishop of Bayeux, half-brother of William the Conqueror, who moved

two hides to his manor of Bramley. After the Dissolution of the Monasteries Henry VIII gave Clandon to his Master of Horse, Sir Anthony Browne, who sold it. The big house is Hatchlands. The church, St Thomas of Canterbury, was built around 1110. The nave has its original walls much reworked for the windows and the aisle. The chancel and aisle date from about 1220, the bell turret is 15th century.

West **Clandon** was a Domesday Book manor. From medieval times the Park belonged to the Westons but Sir Richard Onslow bought it in 1641. The village stretches in a ribbon two miles along the road with ancient houses scattered throughout. The *Bull's Head* is an early 16th century hall house with later extensions. The polychrome brick school next to it dates from 1871. The oldest house is Fludyers of about 1500 ½ mile north. The church, SS Peter & Paul, is probably on the site of the Domesday Book church. The nave is late 12th century, the chancel, 13th century and the tower 19th century. It has some elaborate family pews.

Clandon Park (National Trust) was gutted by fire in 2015 but will be rebuilt. The garden is free. The house was built on the site of an Elizabethan mansion, about 1733, by Giacomo Leoni for Thomas, 2nd Baron Onslow. The fine 18th century interiors contrast with the cuboidal brick exterior. The house acted as a museum for the Queen's Surrey Regiment and Gubbay Collection of furniture and porcelain.

Compton is ancient. There was a Roman house here but the name first appears in writing in 727 when 4 hides of Compton were given to Chertsey Abbey. It is CONTONE in the Domesday Book, a manor of 14 hides held by Brixi before the Conquest. In King John's time it was split into the Manors of Down (north of the Hog's Back), Polsted, Westbury, Eastbury and Field Place, still represented by large houses with these names. Some of the cottages are galetted. The *Harrow Inn* has been licensed since at least 1780.

The double jettied White Hart Cottage is a 15th century house. It was a pub sometime before 1780 and may have been the church ale house. Watts Gallery and Chapel are at Compton. *The History of Compton in Surrey* Lady C Boston 1987 Compton Parochial Council 247p

Compton Church, St Nicholas, has a late Saxon tower of flint and bargate. The nave walls were replaced by hard chalk pillars when the aisles were added about 1160. The Norman doorway (inside the porch), font, lozenge mural over the chancel arch and coloured glass in the east window are all 12th century work. The chapel above the sanctuary is very unusual and its wooden guard rail exceedingly ancient. A Crusader graffito is incised on the south side of the chancel arch. The shingled spire is 14th century. *Compton Parish Church* Alan Bott 2000 72p

The **Cornish Rebellion** of 1497 commemorated by the stone near Henley Fort was sparked by Henry VII's tax to pay for a punitive army against the Scots. It may also be seen as a sign of lingering Celtic independence. The Cornishmen gathered supporters from other counties as they marched towards London. An army skirmished with them near Guildford on 14th June and later defeated them at Blackheath in Kent. The leader, blacksmith Micael Joseph, was sent back to the West Country in quarters. The king still felt insecure. *The Earlier Tudors* 1485-1558 J D Mackie Oxfford Hist of England 1994 OUP 699p

Dapdune Wharf is a museum and the National Trust office for the Wey and Godalming Navigations. It was the HQ of the Stevens family who started as canal managers in 1840 and bought full control in 1912. They were also barge owners and used Dapdune Wharf for barge building and repair. The NT now uses the name *Wey Navigations*.

Town Place was the manor house for the manor (La Dune) cut out of the Domesday Book manor of Compton around 1200. The Victorian house is now demolished but the stable block with clock turret remains as a house.

Effingham was a Saxon Hundred as well as the manor. King Æthelstan confirmed the Abbey of Chertsey's ownership of the manor in 933. Its *~ing* name probably derives from Æffa's people + home. The village is in the line of settlements along the foot of the North Downs where springs emerge from the chalk over the edge of the London Clay. William Howard was granted the manor in 1550 by Queen Mary and became a baron in 1554. The name is best known because the Lord High Admiral at the time of the Armada was Charles, second Lord Howard of Effingham, 1536 -1624. His flagship was the first Ark Royal which is used as the village logo. This Howard was also a diplomat and the patron of the actors who became the Admiral's Men of the Shakespearian age. Effingham Church, St Lawrence, has been much rebuilt. The oldest fabric is a remnant of 13th century window in the south transept. Merton Abbey held the advowson. They annexed the rectory estate, with the pope's permission, and endowed a vicarage to run the parish. Barnes Wallace is buried in the churchyard.

Effingham Common is level grassland with clumps of trees, probably left from time immemorial because the London Clay makes it unworthy of cultivation. To prevent development it was registered as Common Land in 1976. Four properties have commoners' rights of grazing and estovers.

Effingham Junction is the name of the settlement as well as the railway complex. The two railway lines which meet here are the minor line from Waterloo to Guildford and the Bookham line from Leatherhead which also carries trains from Waterloo. There are large sheds which serve as a depot for special trains used to clear the railway tracks of ice, leaves, etc.

Ewhurst is first heard of in 1179 as Iuherst, the name deriving from yew wood. It was part of Domesday Book Gomshall but became a separate royal estate when Henry II hived off the northern portion to William Malveisin in the 12th century. The village stands on the Wealden Clay which was covered by medieval forest. The parish is 6 miles long from Pitch Hill to the Sussex border but only 2 miles wide. The church, SS Peter & Paul, was founded by Merton Priory as a chapel-of-ease to Shere around 1140 so there would have been a village in early times. It has a Norman font doorway and window. It was largely rebuilt in 1838 in Gothic Revival style. Ewhurst Place, the castellated building was a large Victorian country house in Baronial style. It was a Lloyds Bank department during WWII. *Ewhurst and Ellens Green* Ewhurst Historical Society 1995 80p

Flexford gets its Saxon name from the growing of flax. At Lower Flexford Farm there is a retting pond. Flax was rotted to free the fibres which were spun then woven to make linen. The pond has a hard base for the workers. It was filled and emptied by the brook. Flax has been used since the Upper Palæolithic.

Flexford brickworks (formerly W T Lamb & Co) now survives as a solitary chimney stack. The works exploited the top 2 feet of London Clay and the surface loam which were mixed with coke breeze to make bricks variable in colour and used for restoration work.

Flints collected from the chalk pits and fields on the Upper Chalk were much used for buildings near the Downs, making beautiful walls. Flint is a form of silica that filled cavities in the chalk left by soft bodied animals decomposing. The gravel of the pits in the Wey and Blackwater valleys is flint washed out of the chalk during the Ice Age.

The **Ford Farm** fish ponds are used for producing trout to stock angling ponds on the Albury estate and at Syon House for the same owner.

The **Goldalming Navigation** reached Godalming in 1763, as an extension of the Wey Navigation. The rise is 10m/32' from Guildford. In its heyday cargoes were timber, barrel hoops, bark, flour and iron goods. The wharfs closed in 1925. In 1968 the Commissioners off-loaded the canal to Guildford Corporation which passed it on to the National Trust. They now call it (part of) the Wey Navigations. *London's Lost Route to the Sea* PAL Vine 1973 David & Charles 267p

Gomshall was GOMESELLE in the Domesday Book. The village has a picturesque ribbon of old houses along the Tilling Bourne and A25. Gomshall Mill, probably on the Domesday Book site, made flour until 1953. The building has 17th century timbers. It is low because the shafts from its two wheels were horizontal instead of vertical.

Great Kings Wood, NT, SSSI, was planted with oak in the 18th century for coppicing on a 25 year cycle to supply bark for the tannery in Gomshall.

Great Ridings Wood, managed by the Woodland Trust, is a fifth of the 150 ha area of woodland, mostly privately owned. The main north-south track is called the Old London Road. It was probably a packhorse route from the industrial Tilling valley and a drove road for taking sheep to graze on the North Downs. The mound along the west side of it marks the ancient boundary of the Woking and Copthorne hundreds. The area of large forest oaks west of the mound is fairly ancient but the rest is plantation or fields colonised by ash. Woodland predominates here because the wet London Clay makes the land unworthy of cultivation. To the north the private wood overruns the moat of the medieval Great Lee manor house.

Guildford first appears in the will of Alfred the Great drafted around 885. GILDEFORD is the first entry in the Surrey section of the Domesday Book listing the properties as if it were a borough. St Mary's Church has a late Saxon tower though its battlements and most of the present fabric are Norman. The castle, thrown up soon after the Conquest was a fortified mound; the existing stone keep dates from the 12th century; £26 was spent on the castle in 1173-4. Henry III lived here as a child, Guildford being part of his mother's dower settlement. Town Mill was built i

771. There has been a flour mill here
nce medieval times and it has been
e town waterworks. The statue at the
p of High Street is of George Abbot,
562-1633, Archbishop of Canterbury
ho was son of a Guildford clothmaker.
e was important as a conciliator but is
est-known for accidentally shooting a
amekeeper. His tomb is in Holy Trinity
hurch. The cathedral was started in
936 but unfinished until 1961 because
 WWII. The Guildford diocese was
etached from Winchester in 1927.

he **gunpowder** mills were, in their
al phase, the Admiralty Explosives
orks, using steam as well as water
ower. They functioned until 1920
hen most of the buildings were
emolished. The sheds visible from the
eld, beyond the pond, were for cordite
oduction, a string-like explosive made
y the nitration of cellulose. The lane
ast the ponds runs along the ancient
am which powered 16 mills at one
ne. The East India Company started
e manufacture of gunpowder here in
625 but sold up to other mill owners
ter 10 years of floods and explosions.
rimstone (sulphur) was imported.
harcoal (for carbon) was kilned from
cally coppiced wood. Saltpetre
otassium nitrate) was still being made
ere in 1790 by watering a mixture of
oil, lime, ashes and dung with urine! -
recipe bought for £300 in 1561 by the
overnment from Gerrard Honrick.
ter, straw charcoal replaced wood
arcoal to give brown smokeless
owder. 500 tons of gunpowder were
ansported on the Wey Navigation in
873. Latterly the works were owned by
German Company which was taken
ver by Nobel Industries which became
art of ICI. *Damnable Inventions* Glenys &
 Alan Crocker 2000 Surrey Indust Hist Group

allams is a Norman Shaw house built
 1895. It held German prisoners of
ar in World War II. A John atte
ulhamme appears in a 1327 tax list.

atchlands at East Clandon holds the
ational Trust's Cobbe Collection of
eyboard instruments. It has been
ational Trust property since 1945

with the grounds leased for agriculture.
It was bought from a bankrupt brewer in
1749 by Admiral Boscawen for his wife,
Fanny, with prize money from the
Seven Years' War - an admiral received
$1/8$ of the prize money for ships taken
by his captains. He pulled down the old
house and replaced it with the present
one in 1757. The architect was Stiff
Leadbetter and the interior rococo was
the early work of Robert Adam whose
fireplaces and ceilings are still intact.

Heath forms in low-rainfall areas on
sandy soils lacking calcium. Because of
the Tertiary Sands and Ice-Age gravel
deposits north of the Downs and the
Lower Greensand to the south the area
has extensive heaths . Humus does not
gel on the soil grains in the absence of
calcium and humus is needed to hold
the water, nutrients and microbes. Only
a few plants such as heathers, gorse
and bracken thrive. The heaths are
"badlands" caused by forest clearance
from the Neolithic times onwards.
Intensive grazing by sheep, goats and
rabbits up to the beginning of the 20th
century kept trees at bay but silver
birch and pines (and houses) have
rapidly colonised since the 1950s

Heathercourt was built in 1880. From
1932 it was the home of Frances
Stevenson, Lloyd George's secretary
and mistress for 30 years. He retained
his own house at Churt. They were
able to marry in 1943 (in Guildford).
My Darling Pussy (letters) ed A J P Taylor
1975 Weidenfield & Nicholson 259p

Heathstone is a siliceous sandstone
that occurs in the Tertiary Sands and
has been taken for building churches,
with rarely enough for a whole building.
Root fossils suggest it is lithified soil.
Sarcens are isolated lumps of it left on
the surface by weathering.

Heath Mill, near Pirbright, operated
from 1516 to 1950.

Henley Fort opens to the public on
heritage days. It was a mobilisation
depot in the chain of defences from
Guildford to Epping built in the 1890s to
guard against invasion while the army

and navy were scattered across the Empire. It consists of store rooms and offices below ground level, enclosed by an earth mound. France was perceived the likely aggressor but the panic had started in 1871 with a story, *The Battle of Dorking*, published in *Blackwood's Edinburgh Magazine*, which told of a German army continuing to Britain after the Franco-Prussian War. The story was the first of the genre of "What if" war stories. *The London mobilisation centres* V Smith *London Archæologist* vol 2 No 10 1975 *The Battle of Dorking* G Chesney 1997 OUP 44p

Henley Park house was built in 1751 and converted to flats in 1998, after a fire. The Domesday Book records that HENLEI was given to Chertsey Abbey by Azor *for his soul's sake in the time of King William, as the monks say*. The manor was land which included Frimley, Ash and Normandy and reached to the River Wey. In medieval times it was leased to the crown and the rent included 12 gallons of honey. For 700 years courtiers lived at Henley. One was Reginald Bray who found Richard III's crown in the hawthorn at Bosworth. Queen Mary granted Henley to the recusant Lord Montague who lived here and gave a home to priests but was sufficiently esteemed by Elizabeth I to be employed as a diplomat. Vokes purchased the estate in 1940 as a new site for his bombed Putney factory.
The History of Henley Park Vokes 21p *Henley Park in Surrey...* 2012 John Squier 196p

The **Hog's Back** is the part of the North Downs where the bending of the strata is most extreme; the bedding in Seale chalk pits has a dip of 60°. The name was invented around 1800 and first appears in a letter of 1802 quoted by Mowbray Howard in *The Longs of Jamaica and Hampton Lodge*. Gilbert White was still calling it *Guildown* in his diary in 1797. The road along the top is likely to be one of the oldest in Britain. It was *Strata de Geldone* in 1189.

Holmbury Hill, 875'/261ms is part of the Leith Hill range on the Greensand escarpment. The Iron Age hill fort on top occupies 8 acres/3¼ ha.

Holmbury St Mary is a contrived name with *bury* from the Iron Age burh on Holmbury Hill and the saint from the church. The parish was put together after the church was built, from the hamlets of Abinger Sutton, Felday and Pitland Street. Several London families built large houses after the railway wa built and the village is relatively recent in origin. Bargate is the main building stone. The church, St Mary, was funde and designed by architect George Edmund Street, 1824-81, who lived here. He was one of the greatest exponents of Gothic revival and built c restored churches all over Britain and one in Constantinople. His best knowr work is the law courts in The Strand.

The **Horsley**s: see box with Walk 40.

At **Hound House** the hounds of the royal manor of Gomshall were kept.

The **Hurtwood** was originally woodlan awarded to Reginal Bray of Shere by Richard III. *Hurts* is a Surrey dialect name for bilberries. In 1926 the lord of the manor dedicated much of it for the public right to roam. The Albury estate added to the area. The land is still in private ownership, mainly hilltop heath and forestry plantations. Hurtwood Control came into being to limit damag by motor vehicles and is now a charity called Friends of Hurtwood. It has a ranger and numerous car parks. www

The **icehouse** at Hatchlands Park is 20th century and 20 feet deep. Ice wa collected in the winter and compacted in the deep bowl. In Britain ice houses came into use in the 17th century but predate 1500BC in Asia.

The **incorporating mills** of Chilworth gunpowder works homogenised the d ingredients with edge runner mills. The walls are thick and the roof was thin s explosions would go upwards. This wa the main part of the works in the 19th century when steam was used as well as water power. Major explosions took place in 1902 when six men died and St Martha's Church was damaged.
A Guide to the Chilworth Gunpowder Mil Glenys Crocker 1990 Shire Publications 12p

ronstone or carstone is much darker than bargate sandstone. It occurs in the Folkstone Sands of the Lower Greensand, and is locally abundant enough for building. It was sometimes smelted for iron, having 20-30% by weight.

Jacobswell is largely mid-20th century development within the triangle of roads. New houses were built in 1911; previously there were only scattered old houses, most still there. The name appears first in maps of 1812 & 1823 for an area around the crossroads and was first used as an address in 1836 but its origins are obscure. *Jacob's Well - How the name got its village* Jim Miller 1994 57p

The **Junction Canal** linked the thriving Arun and Wey Navigations in 1816. The idea was conceived at the time of the Napoleonic Wars and marketed as a means of avoiding French privateers on the sea route between London and Portsmouth. The Arun Navigation had reached Newbridge by 1787. The Wey Navigation had reached Guildford in 1653. Both were successful but the Junction Canal across the Weald came too late and leaked. It paid for itself but proved a poor investment for its owners. The peak trading year for all three was 1839. *London's Lost Route to the Sea* P A L Vine 1973 David & Charles 267p

Keeper's Cottage in Walnut Tree Bottom belonged to the Onslow Estate. The flint wall has bolt holes for the hares which were bred here.

Littlefield Manor House is a farmhouse with a grandiose name devised by its 1940s owners. The original Tudor timber-framed farm house which still forms the back part was probably built by Walter Hewatt, "billman of the best sort" in the Armada musters. The front part in brick was added in Dutch style probably by Henry Baker, farmer, who was taxed for 5 fireplaces in 1664.

Littleton was the Domesday Book manor, LITELTONE, held by Wulfwy Hunter before and after the Conquest; presumably he was the king's hunter. Most of the old cottages in the village are 17th century: 8 & 9, 22 & 23, Pillar Box Cottage, Long Meadow, Littleton Farm and Willowmede.

Loseley house is open for guided tours on summer afternoons.www Loseley is widely known for the ice-cream which used to be made here. The estate is a dairy farm. It was LOSELE in the Domesday Book, a small manor in Godalming Hundred. The estate has been the home of the More (now More-Molyneux) family since the 16th century. Sir Christopher More, a Treasury Secretary of Henry VII bought the estate in 1508. His son, Sir William More, an adviser of Queen Elizabeth I, built the present house in the 1560s using Waverley Abbey stone after the dissolution. Its muniments room yielded 2240 documents from Tudor times onwards, court rolls etc. As the Mores owned other manors round about, these documents are a most important source for local history. Marrying the 17-year old Ann More in 1601 without her father's permission gave John Donne a year in the Fleet Prison which inspired his epigram "John Donne, Ann Donne, undone", to which we might add "well done" as they had at least 10 children!

Lynchets are steps in ground level caused by soil creeping down to hedges since removed, and creeping away below. They indicate very ancient tillage and may be found in woods and towns on ground that was once fields.

The **Manor Farm** is owned by the University of Surrey as a reserve of land for extending student accommodation, teaching premises and Science Park. The moat suggests it was the site of a medieval manor house. The Domesday Book manor of Henley was probably bounded by the Wey and the top of the Downs so it was probably that manor. From 1359-1633 it was a royal manor held by parkers and the farm is thought to be the site of Guildford Park.

Merrist Wood house was designed by the architect Norman Shaw in 1877 but has been extended and burnt. Surrey County Council acquired the estate by compulsory purchase for a mental institution but World War II intervened and it became a farm institute instead when counties were obliged to provide training in agriculture. 23 students joined in 1945 but more than 1000 now enrol and courses have diversified: horse management, golf studies, sports turf management, landscaping, garden design, arboriculture, conservation, etc.

Merrow, now part of Guildford, is an ancient settlement. The church, St John the Evangelist, has a delightful flint exterior and fine roof timbers. There is Norman fabric in the dog-tooth doorway and it has an early 13th century south arcade. It was substantially rebuilt in the 1840s. The porch is on the north side and has 14th century barge boards and Horsham slabs. The Domesday Book royal manor of Stoke was rated at 17 hides which have to be the Merrow farm land between the Wey and West Clandon, some of it cut off by Henry II. By 1241 the Templars owned part of it. Sir Richard Weston acquired it after the dissolution and it was sold with West Clandon to Sir Richard Onslow in 1642.

Merrow Down is common land used by Guildford Golf Club. It was the site of Guildford Racecourse, 1727-1870, fashionable enough to receive prizes from William III and George I. The track was just east of the chalk pit on the ridge, along the top and bottom of the golf course, crossing Trodd's Lane. The trig point, 3rd order, was built in 1948.

Millmead Lock is the first lock of the Godalming Navigation. Adjacent is the borehole from which part of Guildford's water is extracted

Monks' Hatch was a house name. Hatch was an ancient word for gate or access and the drive would have been one of the ways into the Wanborough farm estate when it was was owned by the Cistercians of Waverley Abbey. Its land spread over the Hog's Back. The stone bridge for the 1931 A3 Compton bypass, was designed by Lutyens with crosses where it crosses the Pilgrim's Way. The modern bridge, opened in 1989, is for the modern A3.

Mount Browne is administrative head-quarters and training centre for Surrey Police, serving the parts of the county not under the Metropolitan Police. It also trains dogs for other forces The red brick mansion was built in 1890 by George Browne, 3rd Marquis of Sligo. He was impoverished by the Irish famine and subsequent problems but repaired his fortunes by marrying Isabelle, daughter of Madame de Peyronnet, Paris correspondent of *The Times'* during the Franco-Prussian War The marquis knew the area because he had previously leased Loseley. *Mount Browne* Surrey Police Headquarters booklet 16p

Netherlands is a forestry plantation of the Albury estate. The tracks are open to walkers. Conifers can be grown because the Netley Heath deposits of sand and gravel overlie the chalk. The origin of the name is obscure.

Netley Heath has hard tracks and several water reservoirs because it was used for a major Canadian camp in the run-up to the D-Day landings in World War II. Netley House was the local HQ. An Admiralty shutter signalling station in the London to Portsmouth chain stood above Abinger. The heath has been taken over by self-sown pine, birch and oak and plantations of conifers. Heath flora is aberrant on chalk but the ridge is capped by a 25'/8m layer of sand and flint gravel, extending to Newlands Corner, which provides acid soil and a geological puzzle. The Netley Heath deposits do not have the layered beds of normal sediments. They may have been dumped by the Wealden ice cap melting after the Anglian glaciation, 450 thousand years ago. It is deposits like this which make the North Downs more wooded than the South Downs.

Netley Park was part of the royal manor of Gomshall which Richard I detached to give to the Cistercian Abbey of Netley (near Southampton Water). It is now National Trust land. The mound of the park pale is visible beside the hard track but when made would have been higher with wooden palings to keep in the deer.

Newland's Corner is one of the beauty spots of Surrey. The name *Newland* appears in a court record of 1497 possibly deriving from when the corner was first ploughed. It may have been a *corner* of the manor of Merrow or West Clandon as their boundaries meet the straight edge of Albury here. Agatha Christie staged her disappearing act at Newland's Corner. Her car was found, with her driving licence and shoes, 30 yards from the road down the cart track to Albury. The *Surrey Advertiser* dated 1/12/1926 reports that people turned out in large numbers to search the area; Silent Pool was dragged.

Normandy may correspond to the medieval manor of Claygate, possibly a subdivison of Henley. The name may come from a *Duke of Normandy* inn. Normandy Manor House is 16th century with a new front of about 1818. It was Normandy Farm leased by William Cobbett in 1831; he died there.

The **North Downs Way** is a modern concoction for walkers designated in 1978 by the Countryside Commission, 131 miles from Farnham-Dover mainly on ancient drove roads. Prehistoric and medieval tracks often used ridges.

The **Old Farnham Road** was turnpiked in 1758 but superseded around 1801 by the more gently-climbing road (A31) on the flank of the hill. The Acts for both were repealed in 2013. It was probably on the medieval road that Alfred the Etheling was attacked by Earl Godwin in 1036. The younger son of Æthelred the Unred, he was lured from Normandy during the struggle for the throne after the death of Cnut. The Saxon graves in a nearby garden held large injured men who may have been his bodyguard. Alfred died.
The Anglo-Saxons Ed J Campbell Penguin 1991

Paddington is PAPENDENE in the Domesday Book, a manor rated for 4 hides in the hundred of Wotton. It had a mill taxed @ 6 shillings probably on the site of the modern millhouse and driven by the Tilling Bourne. *Padd~ing~ton* illustrates the problems of place-name etymology. The *~ton* occurs frequently in place-names and is derived from the Anglo-Saxon for farm or homestead but it appears as PATESDON in 1215 and *~don* or *~dun* usually derives from the Anglo-Saxon for hill. The Domesday Book version has *~dene* which is the A-S for valley. Depending on where the estate was located the topography makes all three meanings feasible but *~dene* is the earliest known form so is taken to be the most likely. *Padda* was a man's name and an *~ingas* name referred to a people in a community sense so *Surrey place-names* takes it to be *valley of Padda's people*.
The place-names of Surrey J E B Gover, A Mawer & F M Stenton 1934 CUP 445p

Peaslake is in Shere parish. St Mark's Church, opened in 1889 as a chapel of ease to Shere in 1889. Hard roads reached the village only around 1900.

Pewley Down takes its name from the manor of Poyle or Puille, a grant of land by William the Conqueror in Guildford. Much of it is covered by chalk grassland rich in wild flowers.

Pewley Fort, among the houses, was a mobilization depot like Henley Fort. qv

Pewley Hill Reservoir was built in the late 1960s. The underground concrete tanks hold about 5m gallons, 36 hours' supply for 20,000 people in Guildford. The water comes from bore holes at Ladymead, Dapdune and Millmead and from the waterworks near the mouth of the Tilling Bourne.

The **Pilgrim's Way** name appears to have been codified by Ordnance Survey for a trackway of prehistoric age along the dry and raised chalk-lands supposedly linking Winchester and Canterbury. In Hampshire it is the Harow Way, sometimes identified with the Tin Road from Cornwall

The **pillboxes** are World War II relics of the GHQ line which stretched from the Medway to near Gloucester to defend London and the Midlands. The line follows natural obstacles such as the Downs, canals and rivers.
Pillboxes - a study of UK defences 1940 Henry Wills 1985 Secker & Warburg 98p

Pirbright is not in the Domesday Book. It was probably detached from Woking Manor by Henry I for his son Robert, Duke of Gloucester. It became part of the marriage portion of Katherine of Aragon. The present Manor House dates from the 16th century but there are records of a house in 1302 and part of a moat is still visible. Pirbright Mill, next door, is documented in 1574 as a Lord of the Manor monopoly, usual at the time; it ground corn until the 1930s. The church, St Michael and All Angels, galetted heathstone and brick, is Georgian but there was a church as early as 1200, deduced from a charter signed as witness by Jordan, parson of Pirefricth (displayed in the church). The large granite lump at the other end of the churchyard is the grave of Stanley the explorer, 1841-1904,.

Pirbright Lodge, on the old Chertsey-Farnham coach road, was the home of Admiral John Byron, 1723-86. He took the Falkland Isles by prior discovery in 1765. As a midshipman he was ship-wrecked in Patagonia and took 6 years to get home. Story has it that he set off to retire there but, at Pirbright, found it wild enough and stayed. His journals provided accurate detail for Patrick O'Brian's novel *The Unknown Shore.* He was grandfather of the poet.

Pitch Hill, 257m/843ft, acquired this name only in modern times, from the dialect word *pitch,* a short steep slope. It was Coneyhurst in the 19th century and Coningeshurst in 1263, probably from *coney* - a rabbit. The trig point erected in 1952 was a secondary point in the 3rd triangulation of Great Britain inititiated by Ordnance Survey in 1936.

Polesden Lacey house and grounds are open to the public - a National Trust property. Polesden first appears as a manor in 1470, cut out of the Domesday Book manor of Great Bookham. The name probably derives from the Anglo-Saxon for *Poll's valley.* Anthony Rous replaced the medieval house in 1630. Sheridan, 1751-1816, the playwright, theatre manager & MP, bought it in 1804. Admiral Geary, the owner in 1884 added to it the manor of Polesden Lacy detached from Mickleham. The present house was built in Grecian villa style by Thomas Cubitt for Joseph Bonsor in 1824 and enlarged in the same style by Ambrose Poynter in 1906 for the Grevilles. Mrs Greville left it to the NT in 1942; her grave is in the garden.

Polsted Manor was created by sub-division of the large Saxon manor of Compton before 1160. The present house is relatively modern. The house next door has Tudor features and may be part of an earlier manor house.

Postford Mill (called Albury Mill when demolished in 1996) was built in 1809 for paper-making which it did until 1875. After this it made furniture fabric then animal feed. It is now a cluster of houses and offices. Another Postford Mill, 100m upstream, owned by the same family made bank note paper.
Paper Mills of the Tillingbourne A Crocker 1988

Puddingstone is a conglomerate with stones bonded by iron compounds, hence the reddish colour. It does not look very strong but when broken the flint pebbles split rather than detach. Used in a number of local churches (Send, Worplesdon) but there is rarely enough for a whole building (Wokingham Church). The geological age is uncertain for the exposures are worked out and unknown. It appears to have been formed by lithification of beaches which became part of the Tertiary Sands and/or ice age deposits.

Quaker's Orchard was the home of Si Adrian Boult. The house is 1750s Georgian with Victorian additions. The land is recorded from 1367.

The **Research Park** belongs to he University of Surrey. The units are let to companies directly associated with the University and share its facilities.

Riverside Park is a pleasant area of grassland, scrub, marsh and open water developed for recreation and conservation from waste beside the River Wey cut off by the A3. It has cormorants and waders in winter.

he **Roman temple** on Farley Heath
as still visible in the 16th century and
as located and excavated by Martin
upper in the 19th. He found a bronze
trip, probably ornamentation for a
riest's wand, with markings interpreted
s the three Celtic gods Nantovente,
aranis and Sucellus. An excavation in
939 revealed an 18 foot square wall
ithin an outer 46 foot square and a 10
cre enclosure. A thousand small coins
ere recovered. There is no evidence
f a village formerly thought to be here.

t Catherine's hill is on the Greensand
dge with St Martha's and Chantries.
he chapel was built early in the 14th
entury as a chapel-of-ease to St
icholas' church, Guildford. It Is beside
e Pilgrim's Way. The river below had
ferry until 1964. The footbridge was
uilt in 1985. The tunnel under the hill
pened in 1849 and collapsed in 1895.
n archæologist dug up 3400 flint chips
n the hill in the 1950s suggesting
Mesolithic habitation. *St Catherine's Hill -
a Mesolithic site* G Gabel SAC1976 24pp

t John's Seminary was built in 1890
r training priests for the Roman
atholic diocese of Southwark. It is
ow a regional seminary and takes
verseas trainees. The redbrick
uilding is in Jacobean Dutch style.

t Martha's Hill is a Lower Greensand
ll. The soft sands contain thin seams
f ironstone on top and <u>bargate</u> below
hich hold the hill together and cause
atural steps in the paths. Just south of
e church the reservoir for Chilworth
sunk in the hill. Several round
ouses have been excavated here.

t Martha's Church, built of ironstone,
of Saxon origin but the oldest walls
ransepts) date from about 1087 and
e chancel from about 1250. It was
rgely rebuilt in 1848. The hill seems to
ave been called Martyrs' Hill in Saxon
mes and the name may derive from
is. In the 13th - 16th centuries the
hurch was under Newark Abbey, the
riest's house being below at Tyting
arm. A memorial to Yvonne Arnaud,
e actress is at the east gate.

The **semaphore** system relayed signals
between the Admiralty and Portsmouth
1822-1831. The signal masts had two
articulating arms and replaced an
earlier system of shutter stations on a
different line during the Napoleonic
Wars. The 6th station in the chain was
the five-storey octagonal tower which
still stands on Chatley Heath. The 7th
was Semaphore House on Pewley Hill,
Guildford, whose flat top is now hidden
by a cupola. The 8th station was on
Bannicle Hill near Witley. A branch line
from Chatley Heath was for Plymouth
via the Worplesdon tower and a station
on the site of the Hogs Back hotel This
line was never completed. *Old Telegraphs*
Geoffrey Wilson 1976 Phillimore 252pp

Send was Domesday Book SANDE, a
manor taxed for 20 hides, two mills and
five fisheries, The present village is a
network of ribbons along the roads but
in Saxon times would have been a mile
away near the church and River Wey.

Send Church, St Mary the Virgin, is on
a slight terrace in the Wey valley. The
chancel dates from about 1240 and has
the original lancet windows on the south
side. The nave was rebuilt in the 14th
century and the timber porch added
late in the 15th. A church is listed for
Send in the Domesday Book,
presumably on the same site.

Shalford was SHALDEFOR in the
Domesday Book, a manor with three
mills, a church and a property in
Guildford. One of the families to own
the estate in modern times was the
Godwin-Austins of K2 fame. The
church, St Mary's, is Victorian. It
replaced an earlier building of 1789,
and medieval and Saxon churches
before that. The sharp green spire is a
distinctive landmark from afar.

Shalford Mill (open part-time) on the
Tilling Bourne still has its working parts
intact - a marvel of timber technology.
There was a mill on the site in 1332
but the present building is 17th century.
It was bought to preserve it by
"Ferguson's Gang" in 1931 and now
belongs to the National Trust. There
are two fire marks above the arch.

Shamley Green is best seen when cricket is in progress; some roads are within the field of play and cottages have to be protected by nets. It appears in v5 of the *Just So* stories and somewhat earlier in a tax list of 1332 which had a Thomas ate Shamele, when it would have been a hamlet of Wonersh. Notables of the parish have been Harry Secombe, T S Eliot, W O Bentley(cars) and Alfred Hitchcock. Christ Church, was consecrated in 1864 as a chapel of ease to Wonersh. The reredos and east wall are elaborately painted.

Shamley Green - a history of the village
Shamley Green History Society 1993 61p

The **Sheepleas** are worth exploring. The chalk soil is on the north-facing dip slope of the Downs and sustains a rich flora, with grassland, wooded parts and scrub. Deadly nightshade and many orchids are found. Roman snails, *Helix pomatia*, abound on warm misty days. *Lea* and the *ley* of Horsley derive from the Saxon for a clearing in woodland.

Shere, one of the most picturesque villages in Surrey, has many ancient houses. The 17th century Old Prison was part of a larger house used as a lock-up. The *White Horse* was a house built around 1500 and became an inn towards the end of the 17th century. The church, St James', built around 1190 with pointed arches in the nave roof and rounded arches elsewhere, may have parts of the Domesday Book Saxon church. Points of interest: four Early English lancet windows, Purbeck marble font of about 1200; south door timber of about 1200 set in the reused Norman arch; an early 13th century oak chest; the squint in the north wall of the chancel for the cell where Christine Carpenter was bricked up in 1332 (recorded in the episcopal register of Winchester); the shingled spire whose timbers may date from 1300; several Tudor brasses; Lutyens lych gate,1902.

Old Houses in the Parish of Shere 1985
Shere, Gomshall & Peaslake Loc Hist Soc

Silent Pool wells up silently from a spring in the bed. The tale of the forester's daughter drowned escaping the clutches of Prince John originated in a Victorian novel, *Stephen Langston* by Martin Tupper who lived at Albury.

Stanley, 1841-1904, famous for "Dr Livingstone, I presume" lived his last years at Furze Hill nearby. BULA MATARI, *smasher of rocks*, was an epithet he acquired wielding a sledgehammer in the Congo. Illegitimate and brought up in a Welsh workhouse, he sailed to America, fought in the Civil War and joined the *New York Herald*. His great journalistic *coup* was finding Livingstone who had disappeared whil trying to prove Lake Tanganyika was the source of the Nile. They met in 1871 at Ujiji. Stanley's 2nd expedition continued Livingstone's work, travellin down the Lualaba 999 days to find it became the Congo, not the Nile. He was employed by Leopold II King of th Belgians to build a chain of trading posts, which became the Congo (Zaire and a catalyst for the carve-up of Afric by European powers. He might be the greatest British land explorer but the savagery of his methods, the political turmoil unleashed and his dishonesty denied him a place in Westminster Abbey. *Stanley: 2 vols* F McLynn 1989

Stoke, now part of Guildford, was the large royal manor of STOCHÆ in the Domesday Book. It was taxed for 16 ploughlands, two mills and a church. Then, the manor would have stretched to the Downs, east of the river, and included Merrow. The church, St John the Evangelist, is ancient but much rebuilt. The oldest part is the 15th C tower of chequered flint & heathstone.

Stoke Hospital is almshouses built in 1796 for six widows who were to be called sisters, have two rooms, firing, 4s 6d per week and a blue gown every two years. The founders were Henry & William Parsons, drapers and mercers

Stoke Mill, probably on the site of the Domesday Book mill, is a splendidly obtrusive brick pile of 1879. It was a flour mill until 1956, having converted from millwheels to turbine in 1915, but the previous mill on the site made pap 1635-1869, and was the first papermil

the area. It became offices in 1989.
Watermills of Surrey D Stidder 1990 Barracuda

Sutton is SUDTUNE in the Domesday Book. Henry VIII inherited it and gave it to his diplomat, Sir Richard Weston, 1466-1542, who built Sutton Place, half a mile from the Manor House. Another Sir Richard Weston, 1591-1652, instigated the Wey Navigation, the first step towards canal building in Britain, and introduced Flemish crop rotation. Sutton was the family seat of the Westons until 1857, since when it has had a series of tenants and owners.

Temple Court, now the seat of the Onslow family, derives its name from the Templars who had the head-quarters for their local estates here.

The **Tilling Bourne** powered up to 30 mills and was a major industrial valley before the Industrial Revolution. Now it has trout farms and watercress beds. It is a major tributary of the River Wey, flowing 20 km/13 miles between the greensand and Chalk ridges fed by springs from both. The highest spring is on Leith Hill. The confluence with the Wey is at Shalford Waterworks.

Town Bridge, Guildford, is aligned with High Street and the Mount which was the old Farnham road. Next to it, downriver, was the town wharf at the end of the Wey Navigation. The medieval stone bridge was damaged by floods in 1900. Its *fin de siècle* replacement had six iron spans but was dismantled in 1983 when the town centre was reorganised. The present pedestrian bridge of 1985 has much of the original ironwork but only two of the spans.

Trigg's Lock on the Wey Navigation is at a point where the river and canal rejoin. The lock-keeper's main function is to regulate the water levels with the sluices. Formerly he would have taken the tolls. The house bears a fire mark.

The **trig points** seen on walks in this book are secondary and tertiary survey points, pillars in stone or concrete. They were constructed in the 1940s & 50s for the third triangulation of Great Britain which had been initiated in 1936. Leith Hill Tower was used as a trig point in 1938 when the primary network was set up across the country using sightings of up to 50 km/30 miles. Most of them are now redundant because GPS is considered to be as accurate. *Map of a Nation - biography of the OS* Rachel Hewitt 2010

Tyting is TETINGES in the Domesday book, a small manor in the Woking Hundred, after the Norman Conquest owned by Bishop Osbern.

Albury Organic **Vineyard** next to Silent Pool produced its first wine, *Silent Pool Rosé*, in 2011 and aims to make fine Champagne-style wines. There are 21,000 vines: mainly Chardonnay, Pinot Noir and Pinot Maunier.

Wanborough was the Saxon manor WENEBERGE of the Domesday Book. Its lord, Leofwin, according to tradition, was killed at the battle of Hastings. It was bought for 125 marks in 1130 as a grange for the new Waverley Abbey. The lay-brothers would have worked it, hence local place names with *monk* or *greyfriars*. Wanborough Illinois got its name when Morris Birkbeck, the tenant farmer, emigrated in 1817 with workers from Wanborough and Puttenham. The church, St Bartholomew's, was a Saxon church rebuilt in the 12th century. Wanborough Manor house was the farmhouse of the one-farm manor. It bears the date 1527 when it belonged to Waverley Abbey but architectural details suggest it was built 1650-70. During World War II it was the SOE Special Operations Executive) training centre for resistance organisers in France; it flits through the espionage novels of Ted Allbeury. Trainees were not allowed to speak English and local people called them *the foreigners*. The Great Barn is a splendid medieval aisled barn. Guildford Museum arranges open days and group visits. Tree-ring data suggests it was built in 1388 but the octagonal pillars were cut earlier in that century, presumably for an earlier building. The barn was in agricultural use until 1988 and restored in 1997. It was never a tithe barn. *Wanborough from White Barrow to World War* G Drew 1993 28p

Warren Farm, Merrow, is said to be the site of the manor house of Stoke.

Waterloo and Postford Ponds appear with 7 mill symbols attached in Seller's Albury estate map of 1660. The lane runs along their dam which would have been built for the earliest gunpowder mills. They are fed by the Tilling Bourne and the Law (aka Postford) Brook.

The **waterworks** at Shalford are licensed to extract up to 30m litres a day and supply a quarter to a half of Guildford's water. It takes water from the Tilling, a clean but fluctuating source and can fall back on the more constant River Wey.

Watts Chapel is spectacular. Built at the peak of the Arts & Crafts Movement and consecrated in 1898, it was funded by Watts and designed by his wife Mary in Italian Romanesque with art nouveau interior. The gesso panels were made at the terracotta works by 74 villagers
Watts Chapel Veronica Franklyn Gould 1990 64p

The River **Wey** rises as two rivers, both called Wey, which join at Tilford, the northern from Alton, the southern from near Haslemere. The main river flows through Godalming, Guildford and Old Woking to the Thames at Weybridge.

The **Wey Navigation** from the Thames at Weybridge to Guildford was the first long artificial waterway in Britain. It was approved by an Act of 1651 but the instigator, Sir Richard West of Sutton Place, had already cut across a loop of the river in his grounds and built a lock at Stoke around 1620. The 15½ route miles have 9 miles of canal segments between stretches of original river with 12 locks. The last private owner, Harry Stevens, gave it to the National Trust in 1964 but commercial use persisted between Tilbury Docks and Cox's (flour) Mill until the 1980s.
London's Lost Route to the Sea PA L Vine 1973

Whitmoor Common is an SSSI with open heath encroached by birch and oak. Five Bronze Age urns were dug from barrows in the 19th century.

The **windmill** above Ewhurst was built some time after 1845 when a previous post mill blew down. It ceased milling around 1885 and was converted into a residence around 1900. The earliest record of a mill on the site is from 1648
Windmills of Surrey & Greater London K G Farries & M T Mason 1966 Skilton 276p

Woking Mill was razed and re-built for residential use renamed Gresham Mill in 2010. It is probably on the site of the Domesday Book mill. Until 1835 it made flour for London from wheat from Guildford market. It became a paper mill with 136 workers in 1870. Unwin Brothers bought it when fire displaced them from their printing mill at Chilworth in 1896; they gave it Dutch gables. Three turbines drove the machinery and water still spews into the weir pond from conduits under the buildings. The D-Day orders were printed there.

Wood Street Village has a nucleus of old farm houses around the green. Tradition has the name derived from a Roman road, composed of logs, across the marsh. It was the West End tithing of Worplesdon parish. The flat iron disc near the corner of White Hart Lane was at the smithy for the wheelwright to put wooden wheels into red hot iron tyres. The village green still has a maypole.
Woodstreet - the growth of a village ed Nicola Smith 1988 Wood Street Village Hist Soc 90p

Worplesdon was the Domesday Book manor, WERPESDVNE, *werpes* being an inferred Saxon word for bridleway and *dun*, a hill. Like the Clandons it was owner by the Brownes (later Lords Montague) in the 16th century and by the Onslows in the 17th. The church, St Mary's, may be on the site of the Domesday Book church. It has a 13th century chancel (Victorian arch) and misaligned 14th century nave. The Jacobean pulpit came from Eton.

The **Worsfold Gates** are normally kept open. They protect the Navigation when the Wey is in spate and only then are needed as a lock.

Ye is pronounced *The*. The old English letter for th was thorn, Þþ. Continental printmakers did not make it and English printers substituted Y. Þþ is is still used in Icelandic as in *th*in and Ðð as in *the*n